# Rocket your child into Reading

# Rocket your child into Reading

**JACKIE FRENCH**

Angus&Robertson
An imprint of HarperCollins*Publishers*

**Angus&Robertson**
An imprint of HarperCollins*Publishers*, Australia

First published in 2004
by HarperCollinsPublishers Pty Limited
ABN 36 009 913 517
A member of the HarperCollinsPublishers (Australia) Pty Limited Group
www.harpercollins.com.au

Text copyright © Jackie French 2004

The right of Jackie French to be identified as the moral rights
author of this work has been asserted by her in accordance with
the Copyright Amendment (Moral Rights) Act 2000 (Cth).

This Book is copyright.
Apart from any fair dealing for the purposes of private study, research, criticism
or review, as permitted under the Copyright Act,
no part may be reproduced by any process without written permission.
Inquiries should be addressed to the publishers.

**HarperCollins***Publishers*
25 Ryde Road, Pymble, Sydney, NSW 2073, Australia
31 View Road, Glenfield, Auckland 10, New Zealand
77–85 Fulham Palace Road, London W6 8JB, United Kingdom
2 Bloor Street East, 20th floor, Toronto, Ontario M4W 1A8, Canada
10 East 53rd Street, New York NY 10022, USA

National Library of Australia Cataloguing-in-Publication data:

French, Jackie.
  Rocket your child into reading.
  ISBN 9780207199264.
  1. Reading readiness. 2. Children — Books and reading.
  3. Early childhood education — Parent participation.
  I. Title.
649.68

Cover and internal design by Louise McGeachie
Cover and internal illustrations by Andrew Joyner
Typeset in 12 on 14 Fournier by HarperCollins Design Studio

**To parents and children everywhere**

# contents

| | |
|---|---|
| **How I came to write this book** | xii |
| **CHAPTER 1** | |
| **Encouraging young children to read** | xiv |
| **Where to begin ...** | 1 |
| **Reading to your baby** | 3 |
| Establishing routines | 5 |
| Holding books | 6 |
| Playing with your baby | 6 |
| Talking to your baby | 6 |
| Making word sounds | 7 |
| Teaching coordination | 7 |
| **Reading from two years of age on** | 9 |
| How playing games can help | 10 |
| Games that help coordination | 11 |
| Games that help focus and concentration | 13 |
| Expanding your child's reading | 14 |
| Reading games | 16 |
| Working out how your child likes to learn | 21 |

| | |
|---|---:|
| **Reading from three years of age on** | **23** |
| How to tell if a child is ready to read | 24 |
| More reading games and strategies | 25 |
| **When to ask for help** | **31** |
| Hearing, vision or coordination problems | 31 |
| Low concentration level | 32 |
| Late talkers | 32 |
| Mixing up words or sentences | 32 |
| Trouble finding the right word | 33 |
| Parents with reading problems | 33 |
| Time-out | 33 |

**CHAPTER 2**

# Encouraging older children to read — 36

| | |
|---|---:|
| **Reading from five years of age on** | **37** |
| Giving children help out of school | 38 |
| Coping with reading problems at school | 39 |
| Reading games and strategies | 41 |
| When to ask for help | 47 |
| **Reading from eight years of age on** | **52** |
| Fun with words and reading | 53 |
| Writing and spelling | 54 |
| Teaching children to find the books they like | 56 |
| When children are having problems | 58 |
| **Reading for teenagers** | **64** |
| No expectations | 65 |
| Finding books | 66 |
| Monitoring progress | 67 |
| Helping build their vocabulary | 68 |
| Helping with spelling | 68 |
| Encouraging email | 69 |
| Providing access to a computer | 69 |

**CHAPTER 3**
# How to teach children to read — 73
## Helping children learn to read — 74
How people learn to read — 75
When should you start? — 76
How do I find time? — 77
## Twelve steps to reading — 79
1: What do words and pages look like? — 79
2: What do words sound like? — 80
3: Teach children the alphabet — 80
4: Make an alphabet book — 81
5: Teach children letter sounds — 82
6: Teach children to make sounds into words — 83
7: Teach children to focus on words — 85
8: Teach children commonly used words — 87
9: Putting words into sentences — 89
10: Putting sentences together and making stories — 90
11: Reading a simple book — 90
12: Teaching children complicated words and sounds — 91
## How to help with handwriting — 95
## How to help with spelling — 97
Breaking words into chunks — 98
Fun ways to learn — 98
Spelling rules — 99
## How to help children write stories — 100
What children get from writing stories — 102
How to encourage children to love writing stories — 102

**CHAPTER 4**
## How to spot reading problems and how to help — 107
### How to tell if a child has a reading problem — 108
### Seeking professional help — 117
- Obtaining the right diagnosis — 118
- Accessing a specialist if a problem exists — 120

### Specific problems — 125
- Vision and focus — 126
- Hearing — 128
- Discriminating between sounds — 130
- Memory and recall — 131
- Coordination — 132
- Eating — 134
- Lack of sleep — 135
- Family issues — 135
- Noise and disruption — 137
- School — 138
- Attention disorders — 139

**CHAPTER 5**
## All children learn differently — 143
### How we learn — 144
- Children learn differently — 144
- Spatial or visual learners — 145
- Auditory learners — 147
- Fast processors — 148
- Active children — 151
- Kinetic learners — 153
- Easily distracted children — 155
- Non-fiction children — 158
- Emotionally talented children and social learners — 161

| | |
|---|---|
| Slow Learners | 162 |
| Slow language developers | 163 |
| Bright but bored children | 166 |
| Children who have just missed out | 168 |

**CHAPTER 6**
# Encouraging a reading culture — 169
## Little by little … — 170
## Secret adult's business — reading together at home — 171
### What and when to read together — 173
## Getting children hooked on books — 178
### All children are different — 178
### Get going to the library — 179
### Don't underestimate children — 179
### Help children read widely — 180
### How to help children find fabulous books — 183
## Book groups for younger readers — 187
### Book groups for littlies — 187
### Reading groups for early readers — 188

## Bag a book from my collection — 190
## About the author — 192

# How I came to write this book

I should probably make it clear that I'm not a psychologist, although I studied psychology at university, and I'm not a teacher, although I've given workshops on reading and writing to children and adults for fourteen years. But I am dyslexic — and I'm the mother of a dyslexic child and the aunt of others — not to mention being the daughter and grand-daughter of several more! You can probably add a few 'great-greats' to that, as the form of dyslexia that I suffer from runs in families.

(Actually I don't 'suffer' from my dyslexia at all. As I'll explain later, my dyslexia lets me do many things I wouldn't have been able to do without it. But children with my form of dyslexia learn to read in a different way from most, and I am forever thankful that I learnt to read before I went to school — if I hadn't, I wouldn't be a writer now.)

My experiences have allowed me to see how reading problems can take over a child's life, so that even when they become adults, they secretly remain convinced that they are dumb. I've given talks in schools and have seen children in the back row suddenly look up with desperate hope when I say that I'm dyslexic; and that, although I can't spell or write longhand easily, I've still managed to write over one hundred books.

*All* children *can* learn to read, but some children learn in different ways. It would be wonderful if a child with a reading problem could be sent to the perfect special education teacher who'd wave their magic wand and say, 'Ah, *that's* why Emmeline can't read!' and know at once how to help her. But it's more likely that if Emmeline is going to learn to read, her parents, other relatives and friends, as well as her classroom teacher will all play a big role too. And the earlier Emmeline gets a helping hand, the fewer scars she'll bear from those years when she was sure that she was stupid.

This is the book I wish had been around for my mum. I hope the information contained in these pages will assist you in learning more about reading problems children experience and offer guidance in helping to correct them.

I have provided some invaluable steps to help teach your child to read and to inspire them on the right path to loving books.

★ ★ ★

Chapter 1

# Encouraging young children to read

# Where to begin ...

Reading isn't just one skill; it's the accumulation of lots of skills that children need to learn, from how to hold a book to how to focus on a page.

Children also need to learn to love books. Learning to read is *always* a challenge, but if children already love books, they'll know that the challenge is worthwhile. All children like stories, whether they're stories about ghosts and monsters or true stories about how bees make honey, but children need to learn that those fairly boring-looking lumps of paper — books — contain magic too.

The easiest (and the most fun) way that children learn to read is by just absorbing the words as someone they love reads to them. That's how I learnt to read. My mum read me the books I loved over and over; even now she groans when she remembers the millionth (well, she says it seemed like the millionth) time she read me, *Bobs' Busy Day*.

Every time Mum read me that book, I looked at the words as I sat on her lap. I learnt to recognise many of them once I knew the story by heart. 'Seven o'clock! Time to get up!' said Bobs. (For those who have never read this thrilling book, Bobs was a large ginger cat.)

I also learnt to recognise patterns in the words.

Bobs is the *cat*.

He is *fat*.

He *sat* on the *mat*.

I learnt to recognise the -*at* pattern, and where the syllable breaks came, and so unconsciously I absorbed how the words were put together. And that is how most of us learn to read. We recognise some words. We recognise a lot of sounds and syllables. And we get more accomplished at putting them all together.

We don't even need to know *all* the sounds in a word to work out what it is. A child who can read 'The *cat sat up*' can work out how to read *catsup* pretty quickly, even if they don't know what *catsup* is. (You can probably read the word *catalepsy* instantly, even if you have never read it before.) So you can read to your child from day one; they'll be learning these skills for years, but now is the time to begin!

Reading to your children is not enough, of course, to ensure that they love books and learn to read easily — but it's a heck of a good start. The earlier children recognise how to put words and sounds together, the earlier they will read. And the earlier they will appreciate the pleasure that books can bring.

★ ★ ★

# Reading to your baby

From day one children can start to learn:
- ★ how to focus on pages and pictures
- ★ that the story comes from those squiggles on the page
- ★ left–right coordination
- ★ how to hold a book
- ★ what words sound like when they are read out
- ★ that books are fun before you go to bed, when you just want to relax or when you are bored
- ★ that books mean love and fun and interest.

No, you are not being a fanatic to think about teaching your baby to read from the minute their puddly blue eyes stare at you for the first time!

They won't be reading *War and Peace* for a while — or even *Run Spot, Run* — but they will be learning things. And even if they weren't, it would still be worth it. Reading books and being read to are part of a child's heritage, one of the most magical things that humans have achieved.

Start reading to your baby when they are a few days old — whenever you can catch your breath and start. I'm serious! While you're cuddling them and feeding them, tuck yourself into a comfy chair with a good book and read bits out to them. No, of course they won't understand the story, but they'll love the sound of your voice. They'll also be learning how language is separated into words and what those words sound like.

Reading time is great cuddling time and quiet time and reassuring time. (I remember when my step-granddaughter was eighteen-months-old and sick and crying. Bribes of ice cream and dollies didn't work, but it took twenty seconds of a story to have her cuddling, contented and reassured.)

Reading to children also shows them that reading is fun — and that by learning to read themselves they will have access to an endless number of stories. But reading to very young children also teaches them the way stories flow and the way pages follow each other. They absorb how words and paragraphs look. This early conditioning really does make learning to read much easier later!

They'll also be learning other things that we take for granted — that along with mum or dad's voice, it's the print on the page that makes the magic and that you turn pages. They will also learn how to concentrate right to the end of a story.

Read a bedtime story to your child every night. If you go out, ask the babysitter to do it for you. If possible, read two bedtime stories every night. Try and make one an old favourite, not only because it will teach your child to recognise familiar words, but also because that book is their friend and they love it. The other book should be one that you think they might love but don't know yet.

Ask every adult in the house to read your child a bedtime story — or at least a chapter of one. This teaches children that *everyone* loves stories and reads — nanna and grandpa and big sister's boyfriend, Animal, who rides a motorbike.

Remember to read for yourself while you are breastfeeding, with a cup of something good beside you and your feet up. You can pretend that this will train your child to associate books with being loved and fed, and that reading is something grown-ups love to do. And this is true, but it may be the most peaceful reading time you are likely to get for years, possibly the only peaceful time, so make the most of it!

## Establishing routines

Have regular times for reading — a story before bed, a story after lunch etc. The earlier you begin to read regularly to your child, the sooner they'll take it for granted that reading is just a fun thing that *needs* to happen for the day to feel right.

When children are fresh and alert, read new stories, or more complex stories, or books like the Dr Seuss series — that teach children to recognise word and sound patterns. When they are tired, read their old favourites.

Don't worry if your child wants the same book a million times. They want this book for a reason: it's reassuring, or it strikes a chord in their lives. And every time a child looks at a familiar book, they are becoming even more familiar with its words. Re-reading books is good!

## Holding books

As soon as babies can coordinate well enough to hold a book, let them handle the book and turn the pages. Board books — made of thick cardboard pages — are great for beginners. So are tiny books that small hands can manage.

## Playing with your baby

Babyhood is the greatest learning time in a child's life. You may not realise it, but when you play with your baby you are beginning to teach them how to coordinate and concentrate.

Babies learn to concentrate on one thing for longer and longer periods of time. Play or talk to your baby until the point where they lose interest. Try to extend their concentration span at least once a day; they will slowly learn to concentrate for longer.

## Talking to your baby

Talk to your child even before they can talk to you. Talk *lots*. Tell your child what you are doing and where you are going. 'Now Mummy is walking into the kitchen ... We're going to the shops ... Look at the apples in that bag over there.' For most children, the more they are exposed to words, the more words they'll pick up, and the faster they'll learn to speak fluently.

Don't talk *all* the time, however. Give your child a chance to respond. Even babies need to be given a chance to acknowledge what has been said — perhaps with a smile or a glance in the right direction or a sound, even if they can't talk yet.

If you want your child to learn as many words as possible so that they can express themselves properly, you'll have to *talk* to them — and of course, reading to them will increase their vocabulary considerably.

## Making word sounds

Teach babies what words sound like.

Speak as clearly and distinctly as you can, so that children learn what words *really* sound like when they are not just a vague slur. Speaking to children clearly makes it easier for them to learn to speak and understand language; it also makes it much simpler for them to understand that c-a-t says *cat*, not just a 'c' and a grunt!

It's very difficult to learn to spell words if you don't know what they sound like. Think about a phrase like *thank you*. Mostly people say *than-ya* or *thang-yu*. A word like this would be easier to spell if it was pronounced clearly — and children need to learn that words are made up of different sounds put together.

When you are speaking to young children, speak as clearly as you can — not necessarily slowly, just clearly. Try to sound out the syllables in words — *chil-dren*, *than-kyou*. It doesn't matter if you don't do this all the time, but do it now and then so children learn what a word *should* sound like.

Try to keep the TV or hi-fi system turned off when you are reading to children. It's difficult for children to distinguish sounds with lots of noise in the background.

## Teaching coordination

To read English you have to be able to make your eyes track from left to right. But some children — and adults like me — never learnt left from right. Children with coordination problems find it much more difficult to learn to read and write — how to start at the left-hand side of the page and follow the words across to the right-hand side. It sounds simple but as I know all too well, it often isn't!

Encourage children to crawl — don't be in too much of a hurry to get them to walk. Crawling teaches left–right coordination.

Play clapping games with them: their left hand on your left hand, their right hand on your right hand, while singing a song. Play hopping games, on one foot and then the other.

Dance the hokey-pokey with them: 'Put your right foot in, your right foot out, do the hokey-pokey and you turn about, that's what it's all about!'

These are all games and all bouncy fun, but what they teach is incredibly important. Children need at least one good bouncy coordination game every day.

★ ★ ★

# Reading from two years of age on

From two years of age children can start to learn:
★ what individual words look like
★ that words are made up of letters
★ what letters and syllables look and sound like
★ that written words make up different types of books, newspapers, magazines, letters from friends and emails
★ how to 'read' a book themselves from left to right by looking at the pictures and remembering the words
★ coordination, focusing and language
★ how to concentrate on longer stories.

Children will also still be learning all the things mentioned in the previous section — including how to focus and track, and what words look like.

The above list is fairly extensive. Do not worry if children do not master all these skills immediately. They probably won't until they are about ten years old, so don't push them too hard. Scandinavian teachers concentrate on developing early language skills in young children and don't worry about teaching children to read until much later than we do in our schools — and they have fewer children with reading and behavioural problems.

Some children *do* learn to read at about three years of age; others won't learn until they are eight or nine or even older, and these children may be just as bright. So introduce these ideas now, but don't worry if they aren't picked up straightaway.

By the time children are two or three they have very definite ideas on what they want to read again and again and again. But they are also hungry to learn about the world. The main problem at this stage isn't that children don't want to learn — it's parental exhaustion!

Persist with the suggestions in the previous section, especially speaking clearly so that children can understand how words are made up of different sounds. Hold long conversations with your child so that they learn to concentrate, and play hand games with them to help their coordination. But add some more games, too.

## How playing games can help

*Playing games is as important as reading to your children.* Games aren't just fun; they teach children too. Playing catch teaches children coordination skills and how to take turns. Chasing games teach them how to judge distance, and so on.

When I think of the games I used to play as a child, it is amazing how many of these very common games were really intense lessons in coordination: bouncing a ball against a wall with one hand, and then the other hand, while clapping in between each throw of the ball; playing hopscotch, hopping on one leg and then the other; and skipping — they were all games that taught you how to move in a coordinated way (not to mention having fun, cooperating with others and getting some exercise!).

Try to play at least one game with your child every day. If you can, play one 'sitting-down' game and one active game. (Car journeys are great for 'sitting-down' games.) Encourage children to play these games together. You'll have to teach them the rules — these days where small families are the norm there might not be a mob of older children to teach them for you.

My childhood was rich in games. I was pretty much a bookworm, but even I spent at least two hours every day doing what would now be regarded as intensive coordination exercises, but to me it was just fun!

Nowadays TV, DVDs, videos and computer games are a major source of entertainment for children — and parents are under more stress and have less time to put together a fund of games to play. (And often children have to be ferried to ballet or sport or music lessons — all good things but they need their playtime too.)

## Games that help coordination

To help teach children how to coordinate their hands and eyes — and how to manage their bodies and just have fun — try some of the following suggestions.

**'BOUNCE THE BALLOON' GAME** This is great fun and an excellent way to get children to learn left–right coordination so that they can follow the words easily across the page.

First, blow up a balloon and attach it to a piece of string a metre or so long. The child lies on their back while you dangle the balloon above them. They have to hit the balloon with their right hand, left hand, right foot, left foot, and then twice with their right hand, left hand etc., then three times with each hand and foot and so on. The child continues until they make a mistake.

**'KNUCKLE BONES' GAME** We used to play this with the knuckle bones from a roast lamb but you can now buy plastic ones — or use small plastic blocks. You throw one in the air and catch it in the palm of your right (or left) hand, you then throw two, and catch them, then three, and so on. Now try it with your left hand, and after that on the back of each hand, not the palm. (Much harder.)

**KARATE AND BOXING** The child punches with the right hand, left hand, kick with the right foot, left foot: it is great for very physically active children.

**TAPPING AND STAMPING GAMES** The child taps their head with the right hand, stamps with the right foot, then taps their head with left hand, stamps with left foot, taps the nose, chin, neck, shoulders all the way down to their toes, stamping the right or left foot in between each action. See how often your child can do it without making a mistake.

**CATCH BALL** Teach your child to catch a ball with the right hand, the left hand, standing on one leg and then the other. Then play catch with 'silly' things (unbreakable, fairly safe ones) like pillows, cushions, feathers, leaves, T-shirts, rolled-up socks — great for learning focusing and coordination skills.

**OTHER GAMES** Blocks, Lego and other construction games are good for coordination as are clapping and dancing games, with lots of left–right–left movement: you can make them up on the spot.

Sing songs together, with actions or try skipping or hopscotch or French cricket. (If you can't remember how to play some of these, find a book on games in the library.) These are all excellent left–right coordination games.

Once you put your mind to it, you'll come up with lots of other games that can be played that will greatly improve your child's coordination (and possibly greatly helping their reading and other learning skills).

## Games that help focus and concentration

These are games where children *do* things. Most of these games teach something. (This is not a coincidence — children have most fun when they are learning and being challenged.)

**TREASURE HUNT** Send children to find a brown leaf, then a white stone or a pink shell or flower or a red book, depending on where you are and what they may find. This game also encourages visual awareness.

**'BIGGER, BIGGER, BIGGEST' GAME** Ask children to sort things by size or colour or shape. These can be real things, like blocks, or as they get older, pictures of elephants, cars, buildings and people.

**'MY GRANDMOTHER'S TRUNK' GAME** Each person adds an imaginary item to the trunk, and then has to remember each one. 'I packed my grandmother's trunk and in it I found ... a carrot, an elephant, a chicken sandwich ...'

**'WHAT'S ON THE TRAY?' GAME** An adult (or friend) puts one item on the tray, the other person closes their eyes and says what it is. The friend adds another item so there are two, then three, then four and so on — a great way to get children to focus, concentrate, visualise and remember.

**SCAVENGER HUNT** Leave a trail of cut-out squares of paper through the house for children to follow, or you could use a trail of arrows stuck to the wall, or any other trail (e.g. uncooked pasta or blue wool). Have a prize at the end — a book you will read to them, or a plate of sliced apple.

Encourage children to play one concentration game and one left–right coordination game every day, with you or with their friends — preferably both!

## Expanding your child's reading

There are three types of books to read to your child when they are very young — long complex ones that have several lines of text on a page, not just a bright picture and a few words, new books they're not familiar with yet, and their old favourites.

Don't push a child to enjoy books that are too complex. You'll soon know if they are bored. But try to extend the length of the stories you read to them, to help them learn how to concentrate.

Let children read to themselves too. No, they won't be 'reading', but they'll be familiarising themselves with the way the words look as well as checking out the pictures.

Let children 'read' their old favourites in the car (as long as they don't get carsick) or read to them before they go to bed or before they have an afternoon nap or simply during a quiet time. They'll be learning the words as well as having fun.

Cuddle children as you read to them, so that they can see the page and the text easily too. (There are, of course, other reasons for cuddling.)

Sometimes run your finger along the line as you read but not all the time, or it'll be boring for you and may make your child feel that you're not concentrating on them and the story.

Adults are so used to reading that we don't realise all the skills needed. It's not just about knowing what the words say. When you read you start on the left-hand page, and go on to the page on the right; you read across the page from left to right, then head back to the start of the next line on the left; and you discover that pages are broken into sentences and paragraphs.

It will be much easier for your children to learn to read if they have mastered these skills *long before* they go to school.

## Which books to read?

First of all, read the books they love — even if this means reading *The Cat in the Hat* one thousand, three hundred and ninety-four times.

If a child wants the same book read again and again, they're getting something necessary from the book, whether it's reassurance or just plain fun. But familiar books also help children learn to read by recognising the words or the syllables in the words and often that is one of the reasons why the child wants the book again — because the book is familiar enough for them to almost read it too.

Secondly, read new books, so that children learn that the world is full of all sorts of fascinating books, not just *The Cat in the Hat*.

Thirdly, read longer books that children will enjoy for the story, and shorter books with very few words on each page. These shorter books may have an identifying picture, for example, the word *apple* next to a picture of an apple. They don't have to be alphabet books — 'a' for *apple*, 'b' for *banana* etc.

When young children read *Diary of a Wombat*, they pick up the key words in the text, even when they are about two or three years old — *slept, ate, morning* — even though some of these might be regarded as complex words.

Most children learn to recognise the words after the fortieth repetition or so. (Yes, okay, reading the same book forty — or one thousand, three hundred and ninety-four — times can be wearing, but whoever said parenthood was easy?)

---

## Reading games

Many of these games won't appeal to children until they are three or even six or seven years of age. Don't worry, if the child isn't having fun, do something else! Too much pressure can cause real problems and may slow a child down too.

**THE 'SOUNDING WORDS' GAME**
    Mum: What's that, Alex?
    Alex: That's a cat.
    Mum, chanting out how the letters sound: It's a c-a-t. (You could try singing it to the tune of 'Twinkle, twinkle little star'.) Cc-aa-tt, Cat! Dd-oo-gg ...
    Alex: Dog!
    Mum, clapping: Yay, Alex!

**THE 'TV WHACKO WORDS' GAME** There's no patent on this as I made it up! Feel free to borrow the idea to sell at school fetes.

Make a series of cards with photos of animals, people and other objects cut from magazines. Label each photo clearly — man, car, bird, cat, dog, house, horse, chair — vary the words according to shows the child watches on TV.

The child watches TV with several of the cards in front of them. (Start with one or two cards and add more as their reading improves.) If there is a 'cat' on the card (labelled with the word *cat*) they watch for a cat on TV. When they see a cat they hold up the card and yell, 'Whacko!' and surrender the card.

The game continues until they are left perhaps with the more difficult cards (e.g. elephant, lion, telephone).

If you don't watch much TV, you can play the 'Window Whacko' game. Make cards of things the child might see out the window (e.g. grass, sky, car, truck, bus, dog, cat). Don't have cards of exotic things like elephants (unless you *are* likely to see one) otherwise your child will just be disappointed.

**WRITING WORDS** The child tells you the word, you print it, and then they colour around it or do an appropriate drawing e.g. cat, house, dinosaur, or grandma.

Make your own picture books. The child tells you the words, you write them down, and then they illustrate the pages. Staple the pages together to make a real book.

These home-made books can be alphabet books — 'a' is for *Annabelle*, 'b' is for *book* — or story books: they tell you the story, you write it, and they illustrate it.

**LIFT-THE-FLAP BOOKS** Get children used to participating in reading with lift-the-flap or pull-the-tab books. These also encourage children to really concentrate on the details in books. (Also, they're fun and often beautiful too.)

**READING REAL THINGS** Read your child interesting bits from newspapers and magazines, e.g. recipes and stories about people and animals.

This is especially important for those children who like real things, not fiction. They need to learn early that reading isn't just about stories and cuddling, but important information about the adult world they want to be part of.

**THE 'STOP AND ASK' GAME** When you're reading an old favourite, stop at a familiar page and let your child recite the next word or phrase to you. No, they probably won't be reading them — just remembering them — but it will teach them to look closely at what the words look like and focus on words on the page.

**WORD AND LETTER GAMES** Start playing with letters of the alphabet: magnetic letters that can form words on the fridge, letters out of plasticine, big plastic letters or letters cut out of paper or cardboard for children to colour in. Make sure that these are lower-case letters, not capitals. It can be difficult to find lower-case magnetic letters, so you may have to hunt around or make your own.

Let children eat words and letters! The ancient Irish hero Colm Cille is supposed to have learnt to read using the letters his nurse pressed into his oat cakes before she baked them. I suspect that this is a true story! Young children are very interested in what things taste and feel like in their mouths — it's one of their favourite ways of experiencing the world. Letters made of bread or biscuit dough that they can cook and then feel and eat may have a real impact.

Give children letters to feel, too — make them out of fluffy material and paste them onto cardboard or cut them out of cheap, off-cuts of carpet. Wrap wool in different colours around cardboard letters, or glue find sandpaper onto them.

Better still, let children help make the letters, and then arrange them alphabetically and into words.

**DISPLAYING WORDS** Write the names of things in your house (e.g. door, bath, bed) on cardboard. Print big, clear, letters in lower case, not capitals. Stick them appropriately around the house at child-height.

Now and then remove the cards and get your child to return them to the right places. Don't stress about this or make it too challenging and if it's too difficult for your child, don't do it. But if they start getting them right, cheer!

The right time to start doing this is when children enjoy it. If they find it too hard, they aren't ready.

**TEACH CHILDREN THE ALPHABET** The 'alphabet song' is an easy way for children to get to know the alphabet. Once they know the song, make a long chart with all the letters and point to each one as you sing it. After a few weeks let your child point to each letter — and clap loudly when they get one right.

No, learning the alphabet doesn't teach a child to read — although it can be useful for looking up things in the phone book in later life — but it does get them used to which letter is which. Learning the alphabet doesn't even teach children what the letters sound like — 'c' sounds like *see*, not the 'c' in *cat*.

So make it clear to children that letters have sounds as well as names. This is a 'b' and it makes this noise: b..b..b..b.. as in *bat* or *big* or *bottom*.

**USE WORD CHARTS** Place word charts on doors and in the toilet at child-height. There are excellent alphabet charts available — fruit ones, toy ones, machinery ones, buy one which has Australian words like 'biscuit' instead of 'cookie' (an American term). There are also great charts of things like trucks or dinosaurs that aren't linked to the alphabet but just have the word printed next to the item.

**COMPUTER GAMES** There are some fantastic educational computer games for very young children that aren't expensive. These games can really help children recognise words, as well as help focusing, coordination and computer skills — and they are great if, like me, you have a bit of a reading or focusing problem yourself and you don't want to pass this stress on to your children. If you are not sure what some letters should sound like, get the children a computer game.

If you don't have a computer, libraries and rural transaction centres will have one that you can use for free or at little cost, although you may have to book time in advance. The local librarian or rural transaction centre manager will help you get started.

Don't be tempted by the costly educational toys that promise to teach your children to read or do arithmetic. Put the money towards a computer instead. Computers do many things; these toys just do one and children soon grow out of them.

**MAKING CHRISTMAS AND BIRTHDAY CARDS** Make simple cards from folded cardboard. The child does a drawing on the front, and then you write the words for them. This teaches them that they too can produce a piece of written work that someone will treasure, and also that spoken words can be written down and recognised by anyone who can read.

**WRITING THEIR NAME** Write the child's name (with one capital letter and the rest lower case) on their artwork, or even on labels and stick these on their possessions, to teach them that a word can both be spoken and written down.

## Working out how your child likes to learn

When my step-grandson Rory plays on the computer he puts his hands up on either side of his head to block out any distraction. But his sister Emily prefers to do *everything* with as many friends as possible — and if there aren't any other children she arranges her stuffed animals to play the games with her.

Children — and adults — learn in different ways. Some of us are visual learners — we learn most from what we see. Some of us are auditory learners — we learn from what we hear. Many children, especially boys, are kinetic learners. They learn by doing and get bored if they have to sit still for long — they learn best when they are moving. Other children, especially girls like Emily, are social learners. They learn best when they can talk about it all with their friends.

Some children may be 'fast processors'. They have to do *lots*. Sometimes these children are confused with children who have attention deficit disorder, but these children concentrate *better*, not worse, and therefore are easily bored.

Visual learners will love blackboards or whiteboards, pictures cut out from magazines and other things to look at, Lego to build and computer games to play. They are often easily distracted by sounds or movement around them and hate having the TV on, for example, while they are trying to concentrate.

Auditory learners at this age will like word games and lots of talking about how the world works.

Kinetic learners will do best with lots of 'bouncing learning' — making letters with water pistols on concrete, skipping while singing the alphabet song, and drawing giant letters in the sand.

Social learners will want to share the experience with friends — or stuffed animals — or teach their dolls what they have learnt.

And many children may belong to more than one category! (There is a lot more in Chapter 5 about this.) But try to fit the learning games you play into the way your child likes to learn — which may not be the way that you do.

★ ★ ★

# Reading from three years of age on

All three-year-olds may not be ready for the steps outlined here. Just try these a bit at a time, and if the child is interested, keep going. If not, wait! And you will still need to follow all the earlier strategies too.

From three years of age children can start to learn:
- that words are made up of letters and sounds
- how to recognise simple words
- how simple words can make a sentence on a page
- how to concentrate on even longer stories
- how to form letters of the alphabet and/or how to tap out letters on the computer
- how to focus and coordinate
- how to start finding the books they like in libraries, shops etc.

A few children will be ready to learn to read now, but even some very bright children may not be interested in reading for years.

Many children can learn to read a few words or a street sign or a simple book when they are three or four, even though they're not able to write well until much later. But don't push your young child.

You can tell if a young child is ready to read — or to learn anything. Children love learning if they are ready to learn that particular skill. If they're bored, don't persist (or at least not with that approach).

Make the whole process as much fun as you can, with appealing coloured or sparkly pens and pencils, whiteboards, blackboards, butcher's paper that you can scrawl all over, letters made out of biscuit dough or cold, cooked spaghetti.

## How to tell if a child is ready to read

Step 1: Get hold of a book with simple text and lots of repeated words, like Dr Seuss's *Green Eggs and Ham*.

Step 2: Read the book to your child once or twice so that they know the storyline and can concentrate on other things.

Step 3: Read the book again, pointing to the words as you go.

Steps 4: Read the book again and again until your child wants another book read or wants to do something else. (Warning: this may take some time.)

Step 5: Look at your child as you read. Now that they know the book, are they looking at the pictures or trying to focus on the words?

If they are trying to work out a pattern in the words — whacko, it's time to really help them start reading.

Most children are able to begin learning to read before they can coordinate their hands to write letters of the alphabet. Don't wait for children to be able to write their letters before teaching them to read, or they may get very frustrated. (On the other hand if they love making letters, go to it!)

Don't expect children to be able to learn very fast and don't worry if they aren't interested at all as they are learning other things instead.

The various steps to teach a child to read are explained in 'Twelve steps to reading' in Chapter 3.

Start at Step 1, and continue for as long as your child is still enjoying themselves. If they seem uninterested, the work may be too advanced for them. If they seem bored, the activity may have gone on too long. Children don't like eight-course dinners any more than we do and their attention span will improve as they get older.

## More reading games and strategies

Playing games is still very important. (See the coordination and focusing games mentioned earlier.) As children get older, these games will become more sophisticated, but they are still vitally necessary. Children need to play a game that involves left–right coordination and a game that needs focus and concentration at least once a day.

Teach children nursery rhymes too, or simple poems, to help them learn how to memorise and concentrate. Having *long* conversations about how the world works encourages concentration too.

**DIARIES** Give your child a personal diary. In later years they may want to write their own, but for now you ask them what they do each day, and you write it down for them, adding photos (where possible) and their drawings of what happened.

This gives your child the idea that words are written down, and because they know what the words will be before you write them and they have the photos or drawings to give them context, they'll find it easier to focus on the words and remember what they are.

**RHYMING GAMES** Rhymes are a very useful way of teaching children patterns in words. Tell them that *cat* rhymes with *mat* and *sat* and your child will work out what *at* sounds and looks like and how 'm' and 's' and 'c' make different sounds.

The more rhyming games you can play with your children the better and you'll probably find that they will start playing them with friends too.

Children catch on to the idea of rhymes very quickly. Children usually pay far more attention to words than adults — after all, a child's main job at this age is learning words!

Say: I have a *cat*,
 The cat is *fat*.
 I have a *dog*,
 He's a big fat *hog*.
...so that your child gets the idea.

Then go on to say:
 Hey, look at *me*,
 I've climbed a _ _ _ _
 If they don't say *tree*, suggest *bee*, *sea*, *key*, *me* then *ttttt ... trrrrr ...* until they guess the answer.

Other simple lines include:
 I swam in the *sea*,
 And was stung by a b _ _

Or in the bath you could say:
Please don't *laugh*,
Jason's having a b _ _ _

As they get more used to this game, just give them the first line:
One, two, three ...
Open the door ...
There is a dog ...
Hi, it's me ...

Don't force these games. If your child isn't ready for them, they'll just look at you blankly or do something else. But if they grin and respond quickly you know you're on the right track.

**SAME-LETTER GAMES** The aim of these games is to make children aware of how words sound and are put together.

For example, help your child find words that start with 'b' (not the letter, sound it out): *bee*, *butter*, *bottom*, *banana*. Then find words that begin with 'c': *cat*, *cuddle*, *cry*. And so on.

**SIMPLIFIED SOUND 'I SPY'** Play 'I spy', using beginning sounds, not letters. Say, 'I spy with my little eye, something beginning with the sound 'd': *dog*, *dinner* etc. You can play this on and off throughout the day. Concentrate on only one letter every day, so that your child doesn't get too confused. It's also a great game to play when travelling in the car.

Be careful with the sounds you choose. Remember *shop* starts with 'sh' not 's'. Keep the sounds as simple as possible.

**USING A BLACKBOARD OR WHITEBOARD** Give your child a blackboard (you can buy cheap blackboard paint and create one out of a suitable surface) and chalk or a whiteboard and marker pens, and let them play with words. For example, your child draws a picture and you write the words underneath, e.g. *dog*, *house*, *mum*, *dad*.

Or you write down a simple word, except for the first letter, and then play 'I spy' until they guess what the first letter is.

*Don't concentrate too much on teaching young children to write.* Most children don't have the coordination to write letters until they are five or six and sometimes even eight or nine. You do the writing and let them tell you what letter to write.

**WRITE A LETTER OR AN EMAIL** Help your child write a letter or an email to a friend or relative. You do the writing, but they tell you what to say. This teaches them how the words they use can go down on paper so that anyone can read them; it will also help them learn to concentrate on a written task.

**TALKING BOOKS** Borrow a couple of talking books from your local library when you're going on a long car journey, or to play during a child's rest period when you don't think they are going to sleep but still need some quiet time.

Most talking books don't teach children to follow the words or provide the pleasure of holding a book and reading it, but they do allow children to conjure pictures in their mind about the story.

Some talking books, however, come in a set with both a tape or CD and a book, and are told slowly so that children can follow the words. Some of my books, like *Charley's*

*Gold*, come in sets like this, but not all libraries have the book/tape combinations.

## Obtaining children's books cheaply

Books are expensive — especially picture books. Picture books need high-quality, expensive paper to reproduce the colour illustrations, and with the best will in the world they really can't be sold cheaply. Often the more beautiful the book, the more expensive it is.

Encourage aunts, uncles, grandparents and other relatives to give your children books instead of toys they already have or an 'educational' toy that may not educate at all!

But there are ways of getting books cheaply.

Hunt for secondhand books at garage sales, or thrift shops and if you're lucky you might find a few treasures. And don't be put off if they're tatty, a battered book is usually a loved book.

Find your nearest secondhand bookshops in the *Yellow Pages*. There are fantastic secondhand bookshops that specialise in 'good' books (and a few bestsellers too) and they often have a great children's section. The books won't be as cheap as those found in a garage sale, but you may get some treasures and some classics that are now out of print, but still magic for children.

Never throw out a book. Take a box to a secondhand bookshop — you'll get the cash — or better still donate them to the local preschool and primary school — and the books will continue to brighten the minds of even more children. Keep the most cherished ones for the next generation. Anyway, your children would probably howl if you tried to dispose of the books they love. If you give a child a book, it's theirs!

---

★ ★ ★

# When to ask for help

### Hearing, vision or coordination problems
If you think that there may be any problem at all with your child's hearing, vision or coordination, contact your doctor or child health centre straightaway. The sooner any problems are picked up the sooner they can be either corrected or compensated for. For example, if your child doesn't seem able to follow your finger as you skim across the lines when reading, or can't seem to focus well on the pictures they may well have a problem with their eyesight.

Don't let anyone except a specialist tell you that your child will 'grow out of it'. (Most specialists will say, 'Here are the things that can help', even if they also say that there is no long-term problem.) Too often parents pick up early problems that are dismissed by health professionals who have only spent a short period with a child — not years. If you have any concerns get specialist attention from an optometrist and/or remedial opthamologist, an audiologist or remedial audiologist, a speech therapist or an occupational therapist — the latter can really help with children who have problems coordinating or concentrating. The earlier children with problems are helped, the better. (See Chapter 4 for further information on seeking professional help.)

## Low concentration level

If children can't sit still and listen to *any* story, even their favourite, or they can't concentrate when you give them simple instructions or requests, like, 'Would you please get the green mug from the table in the dining room and put it in the kitchen,' then it's worth having them checked.

## Late talkers

If your child isn't speaking fluently in sentences by the age of three, it might be time to consult a specialist. Children who learn to talk late or don't speak clearly are at much higher risk of having learning and reading problems. (But don't expect your children to sound like a university professor — listen to other three-year-olds before you start to worry. And some children just like to sit and listen — and may still prefer listening to talking when they are fifty!)

## Mixing up words or sentences

If children confuse words, mix up sentences, or mix up a story when they are trying to tell it to you, there may be a problem.

My son talked about 'effelents' (elephants) until he was five, but I had no idea until years later that this was an early sign of dyslexia. I still call a suburb of Canberra 'Wishfick'. (The rest of the world calls it Fyshwick.) Somehow my brain just can't get it straight.

Most children with this 'problem' will be intelligent and their language will be more advanced than that of other children their age, so it may be difficult to convince anyone who isn't experienced in this area that your child may have a problem. Ask your family doctor for a referral to a speech and language pathologist.

### Trouble finding the right word

If your child seems to be very advanced and articulate and talks all the time, but has trouble finding particular words or uses long wordy sentences instead of the right words, you should seek help. These children may use the word *thing* a lot. They'll know that a word exists for the object they are talking about, but can't remember what it is or how to say it. Again, these children may seem much more advanced than their friends. Ask your family doctor for a referral to a speech and language pathologist.

### Parents with reading problems

If, like me, you have reading problems, ask other adults for help reading to your child or, in later years, help with their spelling or other things you find stressful, and get help from computer programs too.

### Time-out

Ask for help any time you need a break. Small children devour attention — they drink it up as fast as you can give it. Children really need to have six parents, not just two or one!

Finding other adults — relatives and friends — who can spend time playing and talking to your child doesn't just give you a moment of calm and sanity, it gives the children more learning time too.

A friend of mine hires the teenage girl across the road to come over for an hour each day at five o'clock in the afternoon — the witching hour — when children are getting tired and she needs to get dinner on. The teenager just plays with her two children, reads to them, colours in with them. Babysitting doesn't have to be just for when you go out.

# Chapter 2
# Encouraging older children to read

# Reading from five years of age on

Five to eight-year-old children can start to learn:
* how to read (from simple books with one sentence to a page to more complex ones — this will depend on the child. A bright, active child may still not want to 'waste time' on longer stories)
* basic writing (children vary a lot in how well they can coordinate writing)
* that you can have fun with both reading and writing
* spelling and how to write a simple story and other feats of imagination and creativity
* sentence structure
* how to choose the books they like
* more advanced coordination and concentration skills.

By now children will be going to school and learning how to read and write. But there is still an enormous role for parents, relatives and friends who can help to reinforce what's learnt at school by making reading fun. (Even if it gets a bit boring at school, or if they sit next to horrible Egbert who keeps hitting them on the head with his ruler.)

You can also show children reading techniques that are a bit different from those used at school and help if problems develop. (Keep encouraging children to play the coordination and focusing games mentioned in Chapter 1.)

All of us learn and process information in slightly different ways, and just hearing the same ideas in another form or even in another setting and from someone they love may help children understand something that seemed difficult in school. Don't expect teachers to perform miracles. But please thank them profusely when they do.

I can't emphasise enough that if a child *is* having problems, having extra help every day from a relative is essential. And the best way to be able to fit this into everyone's life and budget is for the parent (or a kind friend or other relative) to help.

## Giving children help out of school

You should go through the 'Twelve steps to reading' in Chapter 3. Make sure that your child has mastered each step before you go on to the next one.

If children are happily learning to read at school, these steps will make them more confident learners. And if they *are* beginning to have problems, these steps should really help. If your child is too tired to try extra work, don't persist. On the other hand if they seem distressed at any of the stages, it may be a sign that they are already having difficulties with schoolwork (but they may very well just want to do something else). Remember there is no one way to learn to read.

**HOME READING** Read children stories (or at least a chapter of a story) every day. Be sneaky! Read half a chapter of a fabulous book, then leave it around for your child to pounce on to find out what happens next.

Even when your child learns to read well, keep reading to them. Children love the drama and closeness of being read to. And the books you read to them will be more complex than the books they can read themselves. Try to find out what reading tasks your child is doing at school and go through them at home, but don't be too insistent about this — your child may be totally exhausted and just needs you to read to read a story or play a game.

You can ask the teacher what you can do to help at home. But again, don't push your child, they may have had all they can cope with.

## Coping with reading problems at school

Parents reasonably expect the school to tell them if their child is having problems and if the school doesn't, it may be years before you realise that there is a problem. This does not make you a lousy parent! Just a normal one.

Make sure that every attempt is being made to work out *why* your child is having problems. Lumping all children who have reading difficulties together as 'slow learners' is a crime.

Go through the list of possible reasons for reading problems at the beginning of Chapter 4. It may be that your child has just missed a step or two somewhere and will be fine with a few months help. But other problems *must* be checked out.

Be prepared to help your child learn to read with any of the suggestions outlined in the 'Twelve steps to reading' in

Chapter 3, if it appears that they naturally learn things in different ways from the rest of the class.

There are other things you can do to help your child as well.

**LEARNING SUPPORT HELP** Ask for 'learning support' help from the school if your child needs it — and ensure that they get it. (And don't settle for an hour a week either. Some children need extra help every day to reinforce what they learnt the day before.)

Check that the learning support is provided by a qualified teacher with extra training in this area, not a volunteer parent who may just make the child feel embarrassed and even dumber.

**TOUCH-TYPING** Have your child taught touch-typing! I'd do this for a child as young as three or four if the child seems to be an eager reader, and at any age after that if the child seems to be having any reading problems at all.

It may sound weird, but children can learn to read by learning to write — once they are comfortable with letters and by putting them together into words, suddenly the whole process of reading falls into place.

I'd love to see *every* child taught touch-typing as soon as they go to school. Most five and six year olds really have to work at forming letters, but are quite ready to learn to read. They spend two or three years being bored working at their letters, which can distract them from their reading.

Touch-typing is the best way I know to get a child writing fluently. When you type, you don't have to think about how to form a letter. It is no longer a test of fine motor skills and hand–eye coordination, just a straightforward way of getting those letters onto a page.

Children with major coordination problems may not be able to tap on an ordinary computer keyboard, but special keyboards are available or can be custom-made especially for each child by the wonderful organisation Technical Assistance for the Disabled. I have seen one made that works on a tongue, not a finger, switch for someone who's almost totally paralysed! All work is done free by technical volunteers; you pay only for the cost of the materials and a small administration charge.

## Reading games and strategies

None of the following games will teach children to read — they're just (hopefully) fun ways to build their vocabulary and to practise using words in context. But the keyword here is fun: if the child isn't enjoying it, stop and try something else.

**BUILDING VOCABULARY** Learn a word a day. Get some tapes or CDs of good child-friendly dance music — just music, without lyrics. Every morning or just before dinner, dance around spelling out the words of the day. These words can be simple at first, gradually becoming more difficult — the sort that can't easily be worked out at a glance — like *said*, *says*, *thought*, *choice*, *buy* and *school*.

Write down the words of their favourite song, and then get them to read it as they sing. Yes, of course they'll cheat (if memorising is cheating) — but they'll still work out what some of the words they are singing look like.

Show children recipes in magazines, especially ones with great, mouth-watering pictures. Let them choose what you are having for dinner, it is a wonderful way to encourage them to learn to read the ingredients.

Read out labels in the supermarket: vanilla ice cream, mango ice cream, strawberry ice cream etc. Which one will we buy? Then let the child point out the one they would like.

**STORY-TELLING** Get children to tell you a story. Write it down. Now get them to read it out. Result: a happy creative child, and they get to read something *already* knowing the difficult words.

Read a simple story onto a tape-recorder and play it as your child follows the story in the book. (This is a good activity for long car journeys — but only for those not prone to motion sickness.)

Borrow the tapes of some children's classic books from the local library. There are some superb recordings of books like *The Wind in the Willows*, *Charlotte's Web* and *The Silver Brumby*.

Listening to taped stories is a wonderfully painless way of developing a child's concentration span while they follow long and complex storylines. These tapes are also really good for car trips and for children who are at home, sick in bed.

**HIDDEN TREASURE MESSAGES** Write hidden treasure messages in large, printed letters and stick them on a 'secret' place, such as on the ceiling or inside a cupboard door. Children have to work out what the message says to get the prize. You could write messages like: 'Whoever finds this can have a chocolate', or 'slice of watermelon' or 'sit in the front seat'.

**RHYMING GAMES** Play rhyming games. Refer to the hints for three to five year olds in Chapter 1. Older children (and adults) will also enjoy making up simple rhyming poems, and rhymes are a fabulous way for children to work out how words are put together. You can play rhyming games out loud, or you can give the child a word like *at* and ask them to go through the alphabet and find words that rhyme. This also works well with cut-out or plastic letters. They will put 'a' with *at* and discover that doesn't work. The letter 'b' with *at*, makes *bat*; 'c' with *at* gets *cat*, and so on to 'v' for *vat*.

**VISUAL GAMES** Play 'Word Snap'. Write down fifty or more short, everyday words like *a*, *and*, *said*, *it*, *yes*, *no* and *my* on cards, making sure that every word is written down at least four times. Divide the cards into two, three or four piles, depending on the number of players.

One player puts down a card, the next player puts down another card and and so on. When the top two cards form a pair, the first player to call 'snap' takes the pile and adds it to theirs. The game continues until one player has 'snapped' all the cards for their pile and there are no cards left.

This teaches children to focus and concentrate and also to recognise what whole words looks like. The words can gradually become more difficult as they learn more words.

## A word of warning

Often a child's reading progress will be judged by how well they are able to write letters and words. This can be a lousy guide if your child is having early reading problems. Sometimes very visual children are great at writing and their reading problems can be missed. Sometimes fluent readers can go unnoticed because they haven't the coordination to write or can't work out how to spell or put words together. I learnt to read when I was three, mostly by recognising the words as my mother read me stories. I liked *big* stories with lots of words on a page, such as *Winnie the Pooh* and *Bobs* in particular.

No one realised that I could read when I went to school. It was the tail end of the baby boomer era, with packed classrooms and a darling teacher called Miss Davies who was straight out of teachers' college, with perhaps one-year training.

How could she have discovered that I could read when I couldn't manage to write legibly. Even three years later I was struggling. Okay, even forty-something years later I still struggle sometimes to make my hands obey my brain.

Nor could I put letters together to make words. (Spelling is still a problem, although as the years go by I do slowly improve. I'll probably be a good speller by the time they lower me into my coffin.)

I couldn't even focus on single words on the blackboard and even now I still have to force myself to focus on single words.

At home I was reading *The Wind in the Willows* and the first chapters of James A. Michener's *Hawaii* (which terrified me as it was about tsunamis and even today I still wait for giant waves to hurl themselves up the beach. At five I thought the book was fact, not fiction.) At school I couldn't read *Run Spot, Run*.

It wasn't until I snuck into the library illegally at lunchtime and the principal found me halfway through *Black Beauty* — the original small print version — that they realised I could read. I think I must have been a puzzle to them — and to many of my later teachers also — how was it that I was able to read fluently but not able to spell or write.

Many of them assumed I was lazy or not concentrating, as I gazed out the window and quickly got a reputation for being a daydreamer (which I was). Most lessons were either boring, as I'd already read the entire textbook and knew it all already, or they were incomprehensible.

But although I was frequently punished for not trying, I was never regarded as dumb. Children who couldn't read by Grade 4 in those days were placed in the 'gardening group' and left to pick up rubbish and weed garden beds while the rest of the students learnt. It also didn't hurt that I was good at telling stories. In those early years if the class behaved well, I was allowed to tell a story for the last twenty minutes of the school day — a treat which my classmates passed on from teacher to teacher. Possibly I received better treatment because I was an effective bribe!

It was only as an adult — long after I had lost marks even at university level for untidiness in my work — that I was diagnosed as dyslexic. Like many others in my family (our form of dyslexia is strongly hereditary) I can't focus on objects for more than a fraction of a second before they blur. I can't focus on single words long enough to work out how they are spelt and I read not just by recognising words, but by recognising phrases. I tend to read down the page, rather than back and forth across a line — and if none of this quite makes sense to you, then the 'normal' way of reading still seems very odd to me!

So I'm a lousy speller and I still make major reading mistakes as I don't focus closely on words — near enough is good enough and to me 'bckgrnd' looks the same as 'background'. I once drove to Tathra to speak to a group of children because I'd misread the name Tanja. I have bought cans of potatoes instead of tomatoes, as they had no identifying picture on the front.

But as compensation I work fast. I read quickly, I write quickly, I speak quickly, although I have learnt to slow down so that people without my form of dyslexia can understand me, but sometimes I forget. (When two of us get together we rattle off words like machine guns and usually speak at the same time, an annoying habit of mine with other people, who don't like having two conversations at once.)

I tend to do two things at once too. I find it difficult to concentrate on watching a video unless I am reading or writing letters as well and I like to knit when listening to a lecture.

Most people don't understand that while I do things fast I *have* to do them fast if I am to do them at all. The more I have to concentrate, the faster I have to speak, so that if I have to slow down, I slow right down as I find it hard to think and speak slowly.

Do I have a learning difficulty or a learning advantage? I plump for advantage, although I doubt that many of my teachers would have agreed. Or maybe we should just say I learnt things differently . . . and still do.

---

## When to ask for help

Each term ask the teacher how your child is progressing and find out if they are having difficulties with any aspects of their schoolwork. Ask their advice about things that you might do to help your child learn.

**FALLING BEHIND IN CLASS** If your child is falling behind other children in class, you need extra help. Falling behind now means that they will fall even further behind once everyone is reading fluently and learning new skills.

If your child *is* falling behind, try to work out why and seek advice about what to do next. (See Chapter 4.)

If your child is doing as well as most of the other children, but you feel that they could do better, you may be right.

If your child is bored at school, there may be a reason for this. They may have a learning problem. They may be a fast learner and get bored waiting for everyone else to catch up. They may just have a teacher who doesn't stimulate them or they would rather be playing soccer. However you do need to work out *why* they are bored so that you can do something about it. No child should be condemned to spend most of their childhood bored.

It is important to get help when children feel they need help, even if they are initially too embarrassed or scared to ask for help or don't think it will be of any use. If they are scared or worried about any facet of life or literacy, act!

See also the list called 'How to tell if a child has a reading problem' in Chapter 4.

## How to get a child to read to you

Some schools help children who aren't reading well by getting them to read to volunteer parents. The child reads and the parent helps them out with words they don't know.

This is great for children who just need practice sounding out words. But it's absolute torture for children who are having bigger problems!

What could be more embarrassing than performing badly in front of your friend's mum or dad? Even worse, what if their child isn't your friend at all, but the terrible toad who calls you Dumbo in the playground. And you just *know* that their mum or dad is going to go home and say how glad they are that they have such a bright, *clever* child, not like poor Percival with the learning disability. (And even if only the rare insensitive parent does this — although it does happen because I've heard it too often — the poor child with problems is still wondering if it *might* happen.) Children with reading problems have too many blows to their ego already without adding to them.

So how do you help your child to read? You both read the book together. The adult reads slowly, but doesn't stop when the child stops at a word they don't recognise. This helps the child read whole sentences and scan forward, even if they don't know all the words. It also gives them the confidence to read a page or more.

If the child stops at a word, pronounce it slowly and very clearly, with a space after every syllable so that the child can hear the sounds that make up the word: 'There was the *vol–ca–no*.'

Then you can try alternating paragraphs. You read one paragraph, the child reads the next. This works well because you have probably already pronounced the difficult words, so it's easier for the child to recognise them the next time. If you have already read 'And then the volcano erupted . . .', they can be pretty sure if it's long and has a 'v', it's likely to be *volcano*, and as they already have a sense of the story, there is none of the panic of having to decipher a difficult word.

Also, you can maintain some momentum with the story itself. One of the most frustrating things for a lot of children who are poor readers is that the story is hard to follow because they are concentrating so hard on the words.

If you can get two copies of the same book, this is even better, as the child can follow the words in their own book while you read.

Or you can read a paragraph and get them to then read the *same* paragraph. This can work well for children who are really struggling and hopefully they'll remember enough of the words so that it's easy for them to sound them out. Make sure the paragraph is long enough so that they can't just repeat the words parrot-fashion.

Reading silently together is the best way of all, as long as the child has some fluency. You sit reading your book while the child reads theirs, both silently enjoying it. And if the child can't understand a word, they can ask for help.

Another option is silent reading with help. You read through the page silently before the child does, then tell them about new words they may find difficult. Don't spell them out though, just say, 'Hey, that page talks about a volcano and molten lava and an ogre.' You can either point out the new words before they start reading, or just let the child plunge into the story. Now that they know what the new words will be they'll probably recognise the word *volcano* when they see the 'v'. And if not, they will ask you.

A school in the United States has a great program where childrn read to dogs! Dogs never criticise — and children get wonderful reading practice. Sadly, though, dogs can't help children with difficult words, so this will work only if it's done in conjunction with some of the techniques mentioned above.

★ ★ ★

# Reading from eight years of age on

From eight years of age on children can start to learn:
* fluency with reading and writing
* how to concentrate on longer books that don't have pictures
* spelling more complex words
* sentence, paragraph, report and story structure, and complex punctuation
* how to analyse text to interpret its messages
* how to find the books they like
* how to extend their reading
* a wider vocabulary
* different ways to use their reading and writing skills.

By now children will probably be reading simple books fluently, and they will enjoy having adults read more complex books to them. They'll be adding to their vocabulary — words they'll learn how to use as well as write — and learning literacy skills like paragraphing and how to analyse or put their ideas in order.

## Fun with words and reading

Make time for children to read. A friend of mine has a 'reading and chores' roster — one person washes up or tidies up the room, while the other person reads to them.

Have a set 'reading time' when the TV is off. Encourage reading before children go to sleep, and reading after school as a 'relax' time with a snack.

Most of all, make sure children have the type of books they love! The best way to get children to read is to tempt them with the type of book *they* find irresistible.

**SCRABBLE** You can buy a Junior Scrabble set but children may be able to manage ordinary Scrabble by the time they are eight.

**FIND THE WORDS IN THE WORD** You need two or more players for this game. One person writes down a long word (of at least nine letters). The other players then use the letters of the long word to make as many words as possible in five or ten minutes. For example, the word *gladiator* will give you *I, a, glad, lad, tor, at, it, rot, or, tad, trod, radiator, dial* and so on.

**ANAGRAMS** Rearrange the letters of one word to make another word — *dad* becomes *add*, *bat* becomes *tab*. See how many you can work out.

**USING COMPUTERS** Make sure that your child has an email address. If you don't have a computer with a modem, take your child down to the local library regularly and book them time on one of their computers. Again, this is a fantastic way for children to practise writing and reading, as no one pays much attention to spelling: it's fast, informal, it can be done with your mates and it's fun.

Encourage children to email every friend and relative you can haul up with an email address and to get in the habit of corresponding.

Encourage children to play with the Internet too and, yes, you can do some tactful guiding to watch what websites they *don't* get into, but don't be too overprotective. Steer them away from pornography sites or the terrorists' handbook, but don't make them feel that every site they visit has to be *nice* or even educational.

There are a zillion (shorthand for I've no idea how many) Internet sites and at least fifty are sure to fascinate your child, from watching a volcano in real time to see if it explodes while they're watching, to hunting for the Loch Ness Monster. There are fan sites for cricketers, football players, Olympic swimmers and pop bands. There are also sites that tell you how to build your own computer or a chook shed, as well as wonderful sites aimed at skateboarders and rollerbladers and surfers.

Do a bit of preliminary hunting, then let them choose and zoom away.

## Writing and spelling

Some parents have the bad habit of pointing out their children's spelling mistakes in a written story. This is terrible! A story is a story — not a spelling test! And I doubt that any writer worth their salt would be able to write a decent novel if they worried about only using words they could spell.

Pointing out spelling errors just creates hesitant writers who are scared to increase their vocabulary in case they make a mistake. You should just use a story as a guide to what children can't spell. You should give them ten out of ten for their story (assuming it *is* a great story), then make a list of words that they haven't spelt properly. But *don't* put it at the bottom of the story or it'll spoil the glow the child will get from doing something well. Make a list on a separate sheet of paper, then concentrate on those words in a spelling game.

**HOW TO CORRECT SPELLING** Ask your child to spell a word and then you write out how it should be spelt. If a child has spelt *thought* as *thort*, ask them to sound out how the correctly spelt word is made up: '*th*' + '*ought*', with '*th*' making a certain sound and '*ought*' making a certain sound. You'll have to explain that certain groups of letters make certains sounds: '*th*' as in *think* or *thank* and '*ought*' as in *bought* or *taught*. Then they can put it together.

**HELPING CHILDREN LEARN NEW WORDS** Make a game out of learning new words. Choose a new family word each day — something unusual that they haven't come across yet, like *insignificant* or *excellent*.

Everyone in the family has to use the new word at least once, and as many times as possible, throughout the day. 'Hey Mum, that was a really *insignificant* scoop of ice cream you just gave me!'

**SPECIAL DIARIES AND SPECIAL BOOKS** Give children a diary for new experiences, such as a holiday diary. They can write, draw, do whatever they want as it's *their* book. It will encourage them to write, to think and to be able to express what they feel and see and hear. Photos taken with a cheap disposable camera are a great way to add illustrations. Drawings can also be created using computer software programs for children.

## Teaching children to find the books they like

Children have to be taught and helped how to find the books they want to read. They need to look for books that match their interests, for instance books on setting up a fish tank, magazines about cars and motorbikes, and those horrible thrillers you'd absolutely hate — that they will adore. Often children don't like the same type of books as their parents. (My son says people talk too much in the ones I like.) Finding the books you like is a skill you need to learn!

**LIBRARIES** Encourage children to join a library if you haven't already done so. Let the children choose the books they'd like but you should also select some books for them, so that they have a good variety of books at their disposal.

Ask them if they would like to read to you while you are doing the dishes. (If they read, they don't have to help!) Encourage children to use the local library's computers too if you don't have one at home.

### My child just wants to play computer games!

Many years ago I spent a week with my sick son in a children's hospital. The play room was set up beautifully — toys, a big TV, even a video game, a rare and wonderful thing in those days.

Most children of course clustered around the TV set, and there was a long waiting list for the video game. My son sat with the others to watch the cartoons — TV was a novelty for him as we didn't have at TV set at home.

But one little girl was too feeble to sit on the floor with the others near the TV. Her arms were thin and fragile; two nurses were needed to help her into the play room. They sat her on the beanbag in the corner where she could at least feel part of what was happening. So I sat beside her and offered to read her a story — one of my son's favourite books — that I'd brought with me.

By halfway through the first chapter the children had left the TV and were sitting around us listening. By the next day the TV was off and no one — repeat, no one — was playing the video game and, no, I wasn't hoarse, or not very, because a mum from another country town was taking turns to read too. And my son's father had been sent on a hurried journey back home to get more books. The nurses couldn't believe it.

Admittedly, I read well — I'm a natural ham actor and I love doing it. But that wasn't why the children were listening, although it may have helped drag them away from the TV in the first place. (If you doubt this story, try it yourself: offer to read a really great book to your children and see if they'd really rather watch cartoons — although they may ask you, with some justification, if you'd mind waiting until after the cartoons! But if it's a choice between Chapter Nine of *The Vampire*

*Pirates of Jupiter* that you *have* to read *now* or the cartoons, I bet the vampire pirates will win.)

Children love being read to — especially if it is the type of book they love.

Humans are natural story-lovers and story-readers too. Our history is told in the form of stories; our great religious books are stories. Children *love* books. But they may not love reading them.

There are only two reasons why children don't like reading: they have trouble learning how to read or they are getting the wrong books.

---

## When children are having problems

There are lots of strategies you can use at this age if children are still struggling, but the first thing to do is to work out why they are having problems and to seek help if necessary. (See Chapter 4.)

Talk to your child's teacher or the school counsellor or the principal to get your child some learning support.

Once the child does get extra help, ask yourself the following questions:

- ★ What experience and qualifications does the learning support teacher have?
- ★ Is the child embarrassed or ashamed at being 'singled' out for extra help?
- ★ Is support offered every day, or at least every second day?
- ★ How does my child feel about it? Is the experience positive?

If you are not satisfied, ask the school for contact points for support groups that may be able to help you, for example SPELD which is a support group for children with reading problems. If you can afford private tuition, check the phone book for the names of private tutors. Again, make sure that the teacher you choose is both qualified and experienced.

If you can't afford extra tuition and you can't get enough help at school or feel that your child needs additional help, go through the steps in Chapter 4 to find out where they are having problems. Start working on that area, before moving on to the next stages. But don't push the child too hard as the extra bit of stress is more than they can cope with.

Build up children's confidence as much as you can. Encourage them to take up a sport or a craft or music — something that they are likely to be good at. Praise them for every step forward and generally hug, love and reassure them that they are wonderful and that you and other people think they are wonderful too. Make sure you praise things that are praiseworthy, especially persistence. And don't say, 'I think that is wonderful!' Say, 'You must be so proud of that!' That way children aren't dependent on you or others for a sense of achievement and they can learn to assess their own work and be proud of it.

Provide stress-busters — quiet downtime when you read to them, hire their favourite videos and DVDs, go for long walks, take them swimming, invite friends for a sleepover. Do everything you can to encourage them to feel that life is good.

**HELPING WITH HOMEWORK** Don't nag children to do their homework, help them instead. Time spent doing homework should be enjoyable.

Give them a quiet place to do it, with adequate work space, a good chair, good lighting and no interruptions. Schoolwork can be difficult, and children need the same good working conditions as adults.

Don't use bribes, let them enjoy the work and achievement for its own sake. Don't say, 'If you get good marks this year, I'll give you a bicycle.' But do use unexpected rewards. Often simply celebrating an achievement with a special dinner is better than a gift.

Celebrate small successes and don't make the child feel that they have to achieve some far-off goal to be congratulated. A week or even a day of really working at their homework or an improvement in *anything*, are all worth cheering. And having a child really working at something is more of an achievement than high marks.

But be wary of hollow, empty praise. Make praise specific, not general. Instead of saying, 'You're just an all-round fantastic child', focus on a specific achievement: 'I really like the way you have coloured in that heading,' or 'That story you wrote about the visit to grandma's is so good that I feel we should send her a copy, but I really want to keep the original!' Children have very sensitive radars when it comes to anything remotely insincere, and if they think you are trying to manipulate them with bland, one-size-fits-all praise, it will undermine their confidence even more.

Don't go overboard with praising either. Even if you are pretty sure your child is a genius, don't tell them. If they don't turn out to be a genius, they'll just feel they've failed. And if they *are* a genius, they won't believe you — they'll wait until their efforts are recognised by the outside world.

Don't stress about helping them with their homework! Yeah, I know, I used to find this impossible, especially with spelling and maths. They are both such tortures for me (I am in tears every time I have to work out my quarterly GST) that I am sure I passed on my stress to my son — my body language was shrieking, 'Oh help, we are in for a nightmare here...'

I finally discovered that I needed help, that is someone else to help my son with his maths. Don't get stressed if *you* don't know the answer. Ask.

Do other learning things together, so that children can realise that learning is good for its own sake, not because it's a part of school and will get you punished if you don't do it.

Make Christmas cards together or build your own radio kits or make a bookcase or find out how to keep bees or budgerigars or fish or grow avocados or whatever other fruit the child loves. Life is about learning or relearning is about life (whichever way you put it) and school is only a small part of that.

It can be really good for children to see you cope with the inevitable frustrations that come with learning any new skill. So do something challenging together that you have never attempted before — build a balsa wood model plane or glider, set up a tropical fish tank, make a pair of overalls — it doesn't matter what the project is, what is important is that you do it together and that it is a new challenge for both of you. This allows children to see that you keep on learning all your life and that there are some things that you can derive enormous enjoyment from once you have invested some time and energy into mastering the basic skills.

If you have a problem with frustration and anger management yourself, do something about it now. Don't model fury to your child as a response to meeting an obstacle — adult tantrum-throwers are even less attractive than child tantrum-throwers.

## Confidence is all

---

Often the best thing you can do for children is to give them confidence. About a decade ago I was judging a literary competition. There were a host of entries for just about every section, but for some reason there was only one in the ten to twelve-year-old Poetry Section.

The poem was by a child called Mordecai (well, no it wasn't, but I won't tell you his real name) and it was pretty terrible. But the prize had to go to someone, so on the grand day there was Mordecai lined up with all the other winners, children and adults, and looking as pleased as if he'd won the Nobel Prize for Literature. His family even video-taped the event to send back to Grandma in England, and he probably had his photo taken three times as often as any of the other winners.

But it was still a lousy poem.

Six months later I received a bulky package from Mordecai. He'd written a whole book of poems. After all, he was a brilliant poet, wasn't he? He'd won first prize in a poetry contest!

I started reading with some trepidation. This soon turned to shock. The poems ranged from good to simply stunning. This child actually *was* a poet.

What had changed? His confidence. He knew he was good. So now he no longer had to make his poems like everyone else's. He didn't worry that he was wasting time. He could throw himself wholeheartedly into the joy of words and ideas.

Ten years later he is still a poet. He's worked at it and it shows. He's a consistently superb poet now. And I often wonder what gifts other children never realise, for lack of encouragement.

Most of us are natural storytellers — telling stories is one of the things that make us human, it's the way we've passed down history, religious ideas, moral maxims. But children turn into far better storytellers when you tell them that their work is stunning rather than pointing out all the things they haven't done or have done badly.

---

★ ★ ★

# Reading for teenagers

Teenagers can learn:
* different ways to use their literacy skills
* how to locate and process information
* more vocabulary, spelling, and different styles of writing
* how to find and use the books they love to read or need for study
* how to write different types of long and complex text.

Many teenagers may also need to learn the basic skills that they should have been taught earlier.

Teenagers don't have much time to find the books they'd really like to read, or even the time to read for pleasure, given the pressure of schoolwork and their developing independent social life, and this is a tragedy. Pouring through a wide range of books not only gives teenagers more vocabulary, a better sense of expression and many different views on the adult life they have so nearly reached, but they also provide stunningly good 'downtime' in the stress and turmoil of teenage lives.

A teenager is learning to be their own person — to survive and find out who they are. Sadly parents are often the worst possible teachers for a teenager and you fall into the 'I know best and you will do what I tell you' role all too easily.

A parent's role at this stage is as a support person, not a managing director. You have to be there when they need you and learn to butt out at other times — and perhaps to arrange things so that they get the support they need from other people, whether it be teacher, tutor, or a wider group of friends who share their interests.

The best thing you can do for a teenager is be there when they *do* need you. This probably won't be convenient — they'll want to discuss the meaning of life or how everyone hates them or how quadratic equations are impossible, just as you are heading off to bed or trying to take the cat to the vet or have a major conference in ten minutes. But you *do* need to be there, because if you're not there for them at that one critical moment, the moment may pass.

It can be very useful (as well as a source of great and lasting satisfaction) to set up times when they know that they will never be pushed aside, such as lying across the foot of your bed on Sunday mornings, sometimes with the paper, sometimes without; chatting, telling tales and sharing opinions.

## No expectations

Get rid of your expectations. Children never become what you expect; they have their own interests and priorities. This means that the subjects that deeply interest you, from engines to horses, may not be the ones that your children love, although they may come to appreciate them later.

I worried when my son was young that he was tone deaf because he just didn't like music. He's not tone deaf and he *does* like music, just not the sort that I do, or even the music I loved when I was younger.

It's important sometimes to stop and think when you are helping your children learn, who you are doing this for, them or you?

Most of us have a good bit of ego wrapped up in our children and we want them to do well so that we feel good about ourselves as well as them. Children who have problems reading need help — no question. Children who are not doing as well as they might *probably* need help too.

Are they doing as well as they want to? Or is it *you* who wants them to do better? Are they doing well enough to do the things they want to do when they leave school? If so, do they really need to do more than this?

My brother perfected the art of *just* passing every subject he needed, of *just* getting enough marks to get into his BA course, his university honours course, his postgrad diploma, his MA. He said that any more work than what was necessary was a waste of time. No, he's not an underachiever — quite the contrary. But I suspect he was an expert at cost benefit analysis in his pram!

Children who are bored and unfulfilled will be unhappy; they need coaxing and help to do better. But do make sure that it's their needs you're fulfilling, not your hopes.

## Finding books

Always have a range of books on hand for them to read and magazines on subjects they enjoy. These magazines may well be aimed at adults — in which case rejoice as they'll be expanding their vocabulary beautifully. Also do a bit of book hunting yourself for them.

Have newspapers and magazines around in the holidays or at weekends when they have time to browse. And you can borrow a new assortment of magazines every couple of weeks from the library, and sooner or later one may grab their attention. Sometimes children don't know what they are interested in because they've never come across it.

## Monitoring progress

Keep reading to them, if they're not too embarrassed, but don't tell anyone, not even grandma!

Check up on their essay skills at parent–teacher nights. If they aren't up to scratch, ask the teacher's advice. If necessary, get outside coaching.

Let them feel that you have time for them. You can tell a six-year-old to 'wait a minute', but a teenager needs help *now*.

Discuss things with teenagers — your views on politics, the state of the world, your family. (Remember it's their family too.)

Adults often claim that their children don't talk to them, but often the adults don't talk to their child either and, yes, I know I'm veering away from the subject, but this is a time when children's learning needs careful guidance. And tactful guiding is a much more difficult task than the direct steering you could use when they were younger.

A good intellectual and non-threatening loving relationship between parent and teenager really does help guide their learning.

## Helping build their vocabulary

Drop unusual words into the conversation and never speak down to your children. On the contrary, use the longest most difficult words you can without sounding like a Professor of Literature gone loony. Children get enough 'shorthand' speech from their friends, the TV and mobile phone text messages, but if they're going to learn words like 'prerogative' and 'aberrant', they'll probably have to come from you (or books). And having the TV on all the time tends to limit the words used at home. Try the radio news and current affairs programs instead; they are usually more in-depth, without the gripping pictures to occupy the brain.

## Helping with spelling

Any help you offer in this department has to be very tactful at this stage.

Make lists of words that you know they are having trouble spelling.

You can even buy books of difficult spelling words that many people get wrong, like *receive* and *deceive* that have a few spelling rules: 'i' before 'e' except after 'c' etc.

And if you spot a misspelt word on a Christmas card and get away with saying, 'Hey, I think it's spelt such and such a way,' without the teenager having a hissy fit — congratulations, you have achieved a good (and rare) learning relationship!

But remember, wanting to help isn't an excuse for interfering or putting so much pressure on your child that they can't take it or hate learning. As my great-grandpa used to say, 'Good intentions don't butter no parsnips'.

There are lots of ways of making spelling fun. Have family Scrabble tournaments with decent prizes, such as no washing up for a week, or play anagrams. The emphasis here is fun. If they have to be coaxed, don't bother! You can also encourage them to pin up poems and jokes in the loo, or on the noticeboard for more superior poems!

## Encouraging email

If children don't already have an email address or you don't have a computer with Internet access, take them down to the library or an Internet café (libraries are cheaper) regularly and let them email their friends there.

Suggest that they set up their chat room, but keep it limited to their close friends and whoever their close friends think is really worthy of the honour. ICQ is good for this — you can only join by invitation from those already involved.

## Providing access to a computer

If your teenager loves writing stories, a computer is essential. It doesn't have to be sophisticated, just a word processor with no games, no modem, just a simple machine that turns written work into decent-looking pages. A printer (again very basic) means that they can produce good-looking documents of which they can be proud, whether they be letters, essays, cards or invitations.

Secondhand computers can be very cheap, but be warned, they'll probably be filled with junk — one thousand games if you are lucky, porn if you're not. Get someone who knows computers to clean up the software for you before presenting it to your teenager.

## A success story

I met Janice five years ago when she was thirteen. I had given a talk at her high school. Her teachers whispered to me before the talk that she was dyslexic and still couldn't read or write. They had been trying to persuade her to learn touch-typing and to use a laptop computer, but she was sure it would be no use. She was sure she was dumb and that was all there was to it.

The teachers asked if I'd mind mentioning that I was dyslexic too, even though I'd just had my seventieth book published. So I did, and Janice's teachers coaxed her to talk to me afterwards. I tried to be as inspiring as I could and exaggerated the problems I had at school and have now, and told her that I promised faithfully that if she learnt to touch-type and worked at it she'd be reading in three months. (Yes, it was rash, but the girl was desperate.) I said I'd eat my briefcase if she wasn't!

Luckily she didn't take me up on it, because it was four and a half months before I got a letter from Janice, typed on her laptop, with a few spelling errors the spellchecker hadn't been able to understand and so had left uncorrected.

She is doing her first year at university now, studying education. She wants to become a learning support teacher, and I think she'll be brilliant at it, as she knows what children with undiagnosed problems go through.

I still don't know what Janice's problem was. Maybe she doesn't either, although she'll probably find out as she studies the subject. But typing simply made the whole learning process so much simpler, and whatever the problem she was able to overcome it.

And it's not too late even at thirteen — or thirty — to learn to read. I taught a neighbour in her seventies to read one year when she had pneumonia and was bored. She was amazed and why hadn't anyone said it was so simple! She already had the rudiments, but was just too scared to open a book as she 'didn't know which way they worked!'.

---

Chapter 3

# How to teach children to read

# Helping children learn to read

Hopefully you'll never have to use this chapter by itself to teach someone to read, but if your child is having reading problems, this chapter will help you guide them through the various stages of learning to read, while someone with training and experience does most of the work.

This chapter can also be used to teach children the basics of reading before they go to school. As a dyslexic in the days before special education classes, I would never have learnt anything at school (except perhaps that I was dumb) if I hadn't learnt to read at home.

Now there *are* special education classes, but often by the time a child is diagnosed with a learning problem, they are already lagging behind their peers.

If you or anyone in your family has had reading problems, you'll be giving your children a great headstart if you provide them with some basic reading skills before they start school. It may just be the extra boost they need so that they don't fall behind, even if they process information differently from other children.

And if you have an extremely bright child, they'll lap up any reading skills you can give them a year, or even two years, before they go to school.

Understanding reading basics also gives children extraordinary confidence too and the feeling that learning is easy. With luck that early confidence may stay with them throughout their school life.

The earlier children read fluently, the better. It's like learning to ride a bicycle. And once they've mastered it, they realise how much fun it can be.

The sooner a child learns to read easily, the sooner they can start enjoying books as well as learning about the content inside books and writing their own material.

I talk about children all through this chapter, but all the 'learning to read' stages work equally well with adults.

## How people learn to read

There is no one way to learn to read. Most children are taught to read by learning what letters and combinations of letters sound like, and how to put them together — this is called 'phonics'. Children also learn to recognise words they've often seen before — this is called 'word recognition'. The two processes aren't always separate (or separable).

Once a child works out that *c-a-t* is pronounced *cat*, they will probably recognise 'cat' next time, even if it's in a large word like *catalyst*. And they may well recognise *mat* and *fat* without prompting. Other words are best learnt 'whole' by sight alone. Common words like *said* and *though* and *through* don't follow simple sound patterns and only repetition will help here.

But those aren't the only ways we can learn to read. I have a blind friend who is fluent in Braille. She learnt to read by touch and sound, and some children who can see perfectly well still find it useful to feel furry letters. They are tactile learners.

I find it difficult to focus on single letters, or even individual words; I tend to read down the page rather than across the lines and recognise whole phrases at a time. I'm a 'contextual learner'. I need the context of other words and phrases if I am to understand a particular word.

Very young children learn by the way things taste or feel. Social learners learn best by doing things with their friends and interacting with others. Very active children may find it difficult to sit still and concentrate, but if they are physically doing something, they're able to learn fast and well.

There is no one way to learn to read. All of us do best with a combination of approaches and an emphasis on one way or another, depending on how we process information.

Sadly schools have to teach children in large groups. Very few schools have the money or staff to devote the time necessary to finding the absolute best way to teach each individual child.

Despite this all children do best with some individual help — and teachers usually try to work out the best, most fascinating way to help each child to read.

## When should you start?

Let your child tell you this. Children develop at different rates and if you push them too early, they'll just get stressed and decide that they hate the whole activity. Don't feel that your child is dumb or that you are a failure just because they aren't learning their alphabet as quickly as little Percival next door. Your child will be learning other things, from how to relate to people to the shapes of the world around them. Don't push them.

Children are natural learners. They *like* learning. That's what childhood is — a time to absorb the world. Children love attention too. As soon as they show any interest in reading skills at all, get going (but stop when they are bored). A little, often, is the best way to teach young children.

But if your child is falling behind or appears bored at school, it's definitely time to get moving.

## How do I find time?

When both parents are working full time or if you're a single parent (as I have been), time is the most precious thing in the world and so often you are just aching tired in every bone and fibre of your being. But you do have to make time. An adult's prime duty, beyond anything else, is to care for our young. And it may not need as much time as you think, just good organisation.

Most children can't absorb too much in one go. Try to do ten or twenty minutes each day, but don't miss a day if you can help it, as continuous teaching is important. Once a child has grasped part of the reading process you need to build on that straightaway before they forget it.

Then, if you can, do slightly longer sessions at weekends, perhaps an hour each day so that they can practise what they've learnt. And reading the first bit of a great book is the best way to tempt children to keep reading.

Try to make the whole thing as pleasant and hassle-free as possible for both of you. Give both of you a treat to look forward to each time you sit down. Maybe a box of chocolates that you only dip into at reading times when you can each have a chocolate before you start. Whatever treat you choose, always have it at the beginning, so that you learn to look forward to these sessions, not at the end, so that you look forward to them finishing.

The more skilled children become at reading, the more important it is to keep reading to them. Reading stories reinforces that books are fun and once they have learnt to read they can have even more of these delights almost any time they want to. But it also says to the child: 'Hey, don't worry, I'll still read to you even when you can read yourself, because I love reading and I love you.'

★ ★ ★

# Twelve steps to reading

Don't work too fast through these steps as we're talking a couple of years of learning here, although some children who have reading problems will have almost grasped many of the steps already, so will progress much faster. But don't be in a hurry!

Try to do these steps in order. It doesn't matter what age the child is — each step leads on to the next step. Don't go on to the next one until they have mastered the one before, but do adopt a flexible approach within each step. If your child hates sitting still, work out how to make these steps.

Each child is different and each will respond best to slightly different ways of learning. As their parent or loving helper, you're probably in the best position to work out exactly what they need or at least to experiment to find out.

## 1: What do words and pages look like?

As adults we take how a page looks for granted, but imagine if you'd never seen one before. How would you know which bits were words? And that you read from left to right and then down to the next line?

If children don't know this already, read to them until they do, and point to the words and lines with a finger as you go.

Some children will have problems focusing on words and lines like I did, but that doesn't matter as we still need the general idea of how words flow from line to line and page to page.

## 2: What do words sound like?

Most of us don't speak clearly. Listen to the way you say, 'Come on, let's get you to bed'. If you're like me, it'll sound more like 'Comon, lez get y't' be.' How is the poor child to learn what words sound like, or even what single words are, if they don't hear them pronounced clearly often enough?

You don't have to speak like a Shakespearean actor every minute of the day — just remember to sound out exactly how words are pronounced.

## 3: Teach children the alphabet

Make sure that your child knows the alphabet — lower case, not capitals. Teach the alphabet song if it hasn't been learnt before. (If you don't know it, there are good tapes that will teach you both. Ask at a good educational toy shop or even the ABC Shop — and they have mail order too.)

Knowing the alphabet won't teach children to read (although it'll be useful for finding telephone numbers in the phone book), but it will give them a basic familiarity with letters.

If possible, also teach them to pick out letters on a keyboard. (If you don't have your own computer you can book time on one at the local library.) If you think your child may have reading problems, this is essential, and it's fun to tap out letters on a computer.

## 4: Make an alphabet book

Help your child to make their own alphabet book. Yes, I know there are good alphabet books available, but making one will teach your child so much.

All children like doing things more than just passively absorbing and doing things is a far better way to help children remember too.

Dad (writing 'b' in the book and pronouncing the sound the letter makes — *b* as in *bell*, not the name of the letter): What starts with 'b', Jason?

Jason: b-b-b ... book!

Dad (draws a book): Great! What else starts with 'b'?

Jason: bee!

Dad: Great! (Dad draws a bee.)

If your child is really dextrous, especially if they're an older child, they can write the letter with your help. Let them trace over a lightly pencilled letter you've drawn or colour over an outline; you can even guide their hand.

Gradually as they master the letters, the alphabet book will fill up. (If you are really lousy at drawing, you can cut out pictures and get your child to choose one that begins with 'a', 'b', etc., but drawing is more fun!)

Now take your child through their alphabet book letter by letter:

Mum: What's this, Jason?

Jason: 'a'!

Mum: Great! And what sound does it make?
Jason: apple!
Mum: And this is?
Jason: Um...
Mum: What's that? (Points to the drawing of the book.)
Jason: book! b!

Keep doing this until your child gets every one right every time.

Now make another alphabet book with different words in it — a *bed* instead of a *book* for 'b', for instance.

## 5: Teach children letter sounds

Don't worry about teaching 'a' as in *past* here, just try 'a' as in 'hat'! Play the 'What Does This Start With?' game. You can do this either with pictures or with real things. If you have a very active child, play the game when you go for a walk or they are galloping around the yard. It's also a great game to play in the car, as long as you don't have to navigate through traffic or find your way out of a car park.

Dad (points to a dog): 'What letter does that animal start with Emma?'
Emma: 'd'.

This can either be sounded out or as your child learns their letters, they can say 'd'.

Once the child has worked out what words start with, work on the middle and end sounds.

Dad (pointing to a pool): What's that, Emma?
Emma: A pool.
Dad: What does it begin with?

Emma: 'p'. (This can be either the letter 'p' or the sound, once your child knows what sounds the letters make.)

Dad: Great! And what comes next? What does the middle sound say?

Emma: oooooo.

Dad: Great! And what does the end sound say?

Emma: llllll.

Dad: Fantastic! Let's write them down. (Dad writes *p-oo-l*.)

## 6: Teach children to make sounds into words

Don't move on to this stage until your child knows how to separate words into sounds, and knows what each letter or syllable sounds and looks like. They will also need to learn that 'tr' is one sound, but it needs two letters to write it.

To do this you need either letters made from plastic, cardboard or biscuit dough (at least two of each letter) or a computer. (A computer is better for older children, as it's more 'grown-up' than plastic letters and they don't feel like a baby playing with toys.)

Mum: Okay, Jason, what letter says 'm'?

Jason picks up the letter or types it. If he selects the wrong one more than twice, go back to the earlier steps and revise.

Mum: What letter says 'a'?

Jason chooses the letter (or types it).

Mum: What letter says 't'?

Jason chooses the letter.

Mum: Now put them all together and you've got ...

Jason: m-a-t! *mat*!

Mum: Wow! Fantastic! Now, what else can you put with 'at'?

Jason: 'a' ... no, 'b'! b-at! 'c'! c-at! f-at!

Or try this variation. Make cardboard (or biscuit, bread or cheese) letters or use a computer, and play at putting simple words together.

Aunty Annie: What word will we choose?
Tara: *grandma*.
Aunty Annie: What sound does it begin with?
Tara: 'g'. (Or 'gr'.)
Aunty Annie: How do we write that word, *grandma*? Grr-an-. Then Aunty Annie adds the rest of the letters or sound groups.

Make sure that you use very simple words to start with; it gets confusing if 'a' sounds like too many different things from *cat* to *past* to *ate*.

Here's another example:

Dad: Let's play a word game. This is *mum* (writing down *mum* in clear print). Let's sound it out. What is this letter, Emma?
Emma: 'm'.
Dad: And it says 'mmmmm'. And this is?
Emma: 'u'.
Dad: And it says 'u'. So we've got m-u-m. What does that make?
Emma: *mum*.

Of course Emma already knows that the word is *mum*, but that doesn't matter! Now she knows *how* the letters made *mum*.

Keep doing this with simple, familiar words, words that your child has already seen around the house or on charts or in books: *bed, cat, dog, I, hand, me, see, fly, go, lamp, no, yes, wet, bee, jam, can*. This is a very small list, but once a child can sound out all these words they will have a pretty good grasp of the most common simple sounds.

Now try playing 'Take the Word Apart'. This is where the child knows what the word is and tells you which bits go together to make it.

Mum: Look at this word, *dog*. What sounds can you hear?

Jason: 'd'.

Mum: Great.

Jason: Umm, 'g'.

Mum: Wonderful. What comes after 'd'?

Jason: Umm.

Mum: I think it's an 'o'. Can you point to the 'o'? (Make the sound, don't pronounce the letter.)

Jason points.

Mum: Great, d-o-g. You say d-o-g (the sound of the letter, not the name of the letter) together and what do you have?

Jason: *dog*.

## 7: Teach children to focus on words

Write a word on a blackboard or piece of paper (or on a computer screen or with a water pistol on concrete or in the sand in enormous letters — whichever you think will work best or is handy and possible at the time).

Sound out the word, and then tell the child what it is.

Mum: p-l-a-y — *play*. Now you try it.

Jason: p-l-a-y.

Mum: Now look at it and then shut your eyes. Can you still see it?

Jason: No.

Mum: Open your eyes then and look at it again. Now shut your eyes. Can you see it now?

Jason (unsure): Yes.

Mum: You have a go at writing it now.

Jason copies the word as Mum has written it. (But if Jason can't form letters fluently, skip this step.)

Mum: Okay, let's cover it up. (Covers up her word and Jason's.) Now, write it down.

Or if he can't write yet ...

Mum: Which of these words is *play*? Writes down *dog*, *cat* and *play* (or for a more advanced Jason, *pool*, *pot*, *play*).

Important! Don't try to get your child to write or form their letters by themselves yet. Not unless they are an artistic genius with superb hand–eye coordination who can already draw an almost perfect circle (which is something few adults can manage).

Most children can learn to read long before they can coordinate well enough to write. They'll learn to read far more happily in their early years by just feeling the letters already made for them (in plasticine, plastic or cardboard for example) rather than having to try to write them.

Older children with a reading problem may have even more trouble writing a letter and learning it at the same time. Again, try using a computer if possible with them, that way they just have to learn the letter, instead of having to coordinate their hands and their minds at the same time.

## 8: Teach children commonly used words

Once children have mastered sounding out common letters take them onto the next step — common words. Try and make children familiar with the words used most commonly in our language. Children will need these words to be able to read simple sentences. The sooner they can recognise them, the easier reading sentences will be.

Teach children how to sound these out. Explain what 'th' and 'e' in the word *the* sounds like. But don't worry if they don't remember. They really need to fix in their memory what the whole word looks like, sounding it out is just one way to get them to focus on the word.

Some essential words are: *the, an, a, and, I, am, you, will, are*. The easiest way to familiarise children with common words is to play games with them.

**PAIRING WORDS AND IMAGES** Write *the* in front of all the words on a chart of words and pictures where it makes sense, then let your child read all the words with *the* next to them.

Now cut out pictures of chairs, dogs, cats etc. Write down 'a', then place a cat picture beside it. Then 'a' (dog picture); 'an' (apple picture) and 'a' (banana picture); 'a' (house picture) and 'a' (car picture).

Ask your child to read the list.

Don't be in a hurry! If your children only learn one word a week they're doing wonderfully! If you try to push them too quickly they'll either get bored, learn to hate reading, learn to resent you because you keep pushing them, or learn the word of the day by heart (to get you off their case) but not really understand what it looks like.

Go slowly! And stop if they are the least bit bored or stressed.

**USING FLASHCARDS** Cut out squares of cardboard. On one side paste a picture and print the word under it. On the other side print the word without the picture.

Start with a set of about six words, reasonably common, but slightly difficult words. Don't select long words, just those that you can't sound out easily: *house*, *truck*, *horse*, *cheese*, *honey*. Choose objects that your child really likes — perhaps food, animals or noisy machinery. Don't move on to a new lot of words until your child has learnt these.

If your child is very active, get them to attach each card text-side up to the matching item in the house or outside.

If your child has problems focusing (test this by asking them to look at a line drawing for ten seconds. If the edges start to blur, then there is a problem. Use a computer to write the word over and over until it fills up half the page, then ask your child to continue writing the word. Then do another page in another font and another in yet another font. Then print out a page of that word and use it as a flashcard.

**TRACING WORDS** Write a simple word like *truck* on a piece of paper. Sound out the word to your child and have them trace the word with their finger and say it at the same time.

Cover *truck* with some tracing paper and ask your child to copy out *truck* three or four times, saying the word as they trace.

If your child can't sit still long enough to do this for ten minutes, take them out to a sandpit, write the word in big letters in the sand and have them trace over the letters with their fingers.

If your child has problems coordinating, write the word once on the computer screen and then have them type it out again in the same font, and then again in a different font.

## 9: Putting words into sentences

Get your child to tell you a very simple story, like, 'What we did this morning'.

Dad: What did we do this morning, Emma?
Emma: We went to the pool.
Dad writes, 'We went to the pool'.
Dad: What did we do there?
Emma: We had an icy pole!
Dad writes, 'We had an icy pole'.
Emma: And I went for a swim.
Dad writes, 'Emma went for a swim'.
Dad: How's this for a story then? 'We went to the pool. We had an icy pole. Emma went for a swim.' You read it now.

This sort of story is very easy for children to read, as they already know what all the words will be and what happens next. One story like this every day steadily builds up the words the child recognises, while giving them confidence.

If your child falters, help them with the first letter of each word.

Emma: We went to the ...
Dad: 'p' ... 'p' ...
Emma: pool!
Dad: Yay, Emma!

This also teaches children how to sound out part of the word, so that they can guess what it is by its context.

Once your child is beginning to read more fluently:

Dad, pointing to the letter: Okay, Em, what letter does it start with?
Emma: 'p'.
Dad: And what does 'p' say?
Emma: 'p'. (Sounding it out.)
Dad: 'p' ... 'p' ... 'p' ...

## 10: Putting sentences together and making stories

Dad: Tell me a story, Em!
Emma: Okay! Last night Toby ran away. He was a bad dog. But he came home this morning.
Dad cuts the story into sentences.
Dad: Okay, Em, see if you can put the story back together!

(Again, artfully arrange it the first few times so that it's easy to see how the sentences flow.)

## 11: Reading a simple book

Some of the best simple books I know (but there are many others) are Dr Seuss's *The Cat in the Hat* and *The Cat in the Hat Comes Back*. The words are simple, there's lots of repetition, and the rhymes make it easy to work out the words. They also teach children the sound 'patterns' in words too — like *cat* and *hat* — so that children learn to unconsciously recognise those patterns in other words, and break words into recognisable parts. Not only that, they are charming and funny stories.

But older children will need more mature books or you'll make them feel like they can only cope with baby stuff.

(Remember that their reading skills may not be good, but their comprehension and tastes may be mature for their age.)

I wrote the Wacky Family series to entice beginning readers. But you can also use a page or two from almost any good book; that is, a book that you think children will really want to read. Always choose a book suitable for the child's age group, not a baby book because it's simple.

But before you ask your child to read the book, go through the page and pick out any words they may not know. Get them familiar with all the words, THEN ask them to read the page.

Once a child is a confident reader they'll happily just skip over words they don't know. By the time they've seen the unknown word three or four times they'll have learnt it and worked out what it means from its context. Children *need* books that have words they don't know. But a beginning reader will find too many unfamiliar words off putting.

## 12: Teaching children complicated words and sounds

Once children have mastered how single letters sound and can put them into words and read them, they can start learning how two or more letters together sound.

**MAKING A MOO BOOK** This is a more sophisticated alphabet book and should only be moved onto when your child is comfortable with making simple letter sounds, like 'b' and 'c'.

It's best to make your own Moo book, rather than look for a similar book to buy. Most children learn best by doing things, and you'll also be using words that your child knows.

Look for words where the same two letters together make a different sound from that letter by itself. Or one letter makes a different sound when combined with other letters. These include:

'oo' as in *moo*
'a' as in *fast*
'ee' as in *street*
'ph' as in *phone*
'ou' as in *house*
'igh' as in *tight*
'ay' as in *play*
'y' as in *family*

Start with words containing 'oo' that make the sound 'oo' as in *moo*. Then work through the different words so that you have a 'chapter' for each of them.

**PLAYING THE ENDING GAME** Pick an ending and then write out a list of words that can have that ending added to them.

For 's' you might have: *dog, cat, horse, car, truck, phone, bath, sky*.

Dad: What happens if we add an 's' to all these words?
Emma: dogs ... cats ...
Dad: Lots of dogs and lots of cats!

Keep going down the list. This can be either written or spoken. But when you get to *sky* say, 'No, this is a funny one. It becomes *skies* with an 'ies' ending. Sometimes when a word ends in 'y' it becomes 'ies' when you add an 's'.

Make other lists for words with endings like '-ing', '-less', '-ful' and '-ed'.

**READING COMPLEX STORIES** Read more complex stories. Don't worry that some of the words may be unfamiliar — this is the way children learn new words! If the story is exciting enough, they'll work out what the word means from the context — or ask you! If your child doesn't ask you what a word means at least several times a week, encourage them to. Use a word in conversation that you're pretty sure they won't know, 'You're a perceptive child!' Then ask, 'Do you know what perceptive means?' When they shake their head say, 'It means you're really good at seeing things and working things out.'

Do this at least once a day until they're comfortable asking you the meaning of other words they come across.

## Important!: Do not try all these at once!

Just go slowly and steadily and wait until your child has mastered one task before you go on to the next.

And if your child has real problems at any stage, get some help. If children can't put two sounds together, they may need help from a speech pathologist or audiologist to even be able to disinguish the sounds! If they can't concentrate, they may need help from an occupational therapist, and so on. Most difficulties can be overcome quickly by a trained specialist.

Keep revising too and go back over what they have already learnt. And practise *regularly*! Ten minutes every day is perfect. Keep a nice continuous process, so that your child has no chance to forget what they learnt before.

On no account say, 'But you *know* that, Jason!' when he hesitates or stumbles over something that he seemed to master previously. Clearly, the child *doesn't* know it! So you need to teach it to him again.

---

# How to help with handwriting

Learning to write is one of the hardest tasks we will ever do. The more you can help the better. Make sure your child has a pencil that fits their hand comfortably. A very thick one may be hard to hold, and a thin one too difficult to coordinate!

Give them lined paper, but also use a ruler to mark out diagonal lines very faintly to help them get the right slope to the letters.

If your child presses too hard, buy some carbon paper at the newsagents. Put it under their work to show them how hard they press and encourage them to use less force.

Tell your child to pull not push the pencil across the page. Write a few words and you'll see what I mean. Left-handed children may find it hard to pull unless they twist their hand around. Give them a pencil that flows easily across the page to make writing easier. In fact do this for right-handed children too!

Write words as neatly as you can, then put tracing paper over that page and ask your child to trace the words. When they have done that, ask them to write the words themselves.

But remember, most children can learn to read and write before they can coordinate their hands well enough to write clearly! And children who have problems may find it much easier to tap out words on a computer keyboard than try to read and make letters at the same time.

It's more important for a child to learn to read and write (or type) early than it is for them to develop copperplate writing.

# How to help with spelling

If children are having trouble spelling — and I don't mean just shrieking, 'I can't do it! I can't do it!' sometimes when they try to do their homework fast so they can watch TV — you need to find out why.

Are they having trouble hearing the sounds in each word?

Are they having problems focusing on the words? Or breaking the words up into parts? Or ... Well, I could write another book on this aspect alone.

If possible, seek expert advice from a special education teacher to work out which part of the spelling process is the problem.

Following are some useful ways to help any child with their spelling. Choose the strategies that your child finds the most useful.

But don't try to teach them all at once! Let your child practise examples of one rule for a few minutes every couple of days for two weeks before going on to another rule. A little spelling practice every day or every second day works best rather than a great whack at weekends as your child gets bored or frustrated because they can't concentrate that long.

Always revise a few words before you add new ones and try to make the activity sessions interesting: combine a few methods each time and always include one fun session, e.g. spelling with water pistols, singing a new word, playing Word Snap, using a computer, or sprinkling hundreds and thousands into word shapes.

### Breaking words into chunks

First, ask children to say words clearly, emphasising all the sounds. Make sure that they can pronounce each word correctly and pronounce every syllable in the word, e.g. *beau-ti-ful*, *ex-cel-lent*.

Then ask them to use coloured pencils to find little words in big words. Finding the 'on' in 'conceive' and circling it in red can help children break the word down into more manageable bits.

You can try making letters out of cardboard (or biscuit dough or cut-up rockmelon), and asking children to add endings (suffixes) to words: *make*, *makes*, *making*. Or they could add beginnings (prefixes): *unmake*. (You'll find common prefixes and suffixes in any good dictionary.)

### Fun ways to learn

Sing difficult words to silly tunes, over and over until children learn them like a song, or have them write a word six times with a water pistol on six different surfaces — the garage wall, the front path, the patio floor, the bath, the shower curtain, the front steps etc. (No, not on their little brother.) Give them lists of words that have the same combinations of letters and sounds, so they learn that these all follow the same rule: *train, pain, brain, main, again; tree, keen, bee, fee, green.*

Play 'Word Snap' with common words like *is*, *but* and *said* so that children remember what the words they have to use all the time look like.

If children find a particular word hard, show them how to find a clever way to remember it. For example:

*pigeon*: 'Help! there's a pig chasing the pigeon.'

*write*: Write a 'w' when you write.

*kick*: Make the 'k' into a picture of a child kicking.

## Spelling rules

Teach children simple spelling rules:

★ The 'i' before 'e' except after 'c'. Provide examples: *receive, believe.*
★ The fairy 'e' (often called the silent 'e'). When there's an 'e' at the end of a word, the fairy 'e' makes the vowel in the word say its own name, so *rat* becomes *rate* because the fairy 'e' makes the 'a' say its own name. And *cut* becomes *cute*, *hat* becomes *hate*, *kit* becomes *kite*, *not* becomes *note* (The vowels are a, e, i, o, u.)
★ When two vowels go walking, the first one does the talking. So in *dream* you sound the 'e', in *road* you say the 'o'.
★ Drop the 'e' if you add an 'ing', so *hope* becomes *hoping*.
★ A little vowel means that the next letter has to work twice as hard if you are building up a word. So *skip* becomes *skipping* because the little 'i' makes 'p' do twice as much work.

★ ★ ★

# How to help children write stories

I met Gavin two years ago at a high school. I'd been asked to give a workshop for the keenest creative writing students and Gavin, who was definitely not in the top set, asked the librarian if he could come too. She asked me if I minded having one more student join the group and I said, 'Whacko, the more the better ...'

Gavin didn't participate in the workshop but he didn't look bored either. He frowned now and then as if he were working things out, and then nodded with enormous concentration.

Gavin stayed behind when the others left and asked if I'd mind having a look at his story. I said I would, expecting a few pages to peruse. He fished out a great wad of paper from his sports bag.

I blinked.

'It's only eighty-six thousand words so far,' he said. 'I think I'm about a third of the way through. I wrote another story last holidays that was one hundred and twenty thousand words but this one is better.'

I began reading. On the first page one decapitation and a space carrier with all its passengers blown up. No more murders until page three.

'I didn't want to show it to any of the teachers,' he said. 'They'd think I was weird. I want to write books like Stephen King when I leave school.'

It was superb writing — clear, direct, well paced. Okay, it was full of blood and sex, but there was nothing kinky, nothing so dark that I was afraid he was writing to work out some horror at home.

This child just liked a good, bloodthirsty thriller — a taste shared by a large part of the male (and a smaller but still significant proportion of the female) population, and that will probably make him a multimillionaire when I'll be counting my cents to see if I can buy an extra scone when I'm eighty.

His story wasn't at a professional standard yet — you don't get that sort of polish at fourteen — but at the rate he was writing and really working at his writing, I expect to see his work on the airport bookshop shelves within a few years.

I tried to persuade him to show his teachers; he refused. I had a chat to his teachers and told them what he'd written, and why he hadn't shown it to them. One said automatically, 'Well, he was probably right. I don't see why boys want to write that stuff.' But by the end of lunch the rest of us had persuaded her otherwise.

Why expect children to write 'nice' stories when they don't want to read 'nice' books or watch 'nice' movies, and their taste is so widely shared?

I hope that they persuaded him to show them his work. I think they must have. He hasn't emailed me his new book so I suppose he has another audience and helpers now. But I do sometimes wonder how many other boys are bored and under-performing because they are expected to be something they are not.

## What children get from writing stories

*Fun*. Writing stories is like riding a bicycle — hard work at first, but once you are used to it, delightful!

*Word skills*. How to use words they've heard and put words together.

*Logical thought processes*. How to think clearly and logically and put thoughts in the best order for people to understand them.

Even if your child stops writing fiction at twelve, they'll have learnt skills that will help them write anything from a report to an instruction manual to a critical essay.

## How to encourage children to love writing stories

**A STORY IS NOT A SPELLING TEST!** Don't worry if children can't spell the words in their story! And don't correct them either or children will become too inhibited to keep writing! Just make a private note of the words that are badly spelt so that you can help them with them later — much, much later — and very, very discreetly!

**LET THEM RANGE!** Let your children write about what *they* want to write about — this is supposed to be fun, not a way to turn them into a junior Shakespeare. And if they do turn into a junior Shakespeare they are best left to experiment and find their own voice.

**DON'T WORRY IF IT'S A LOUSY STORY!** *Of course* it could be lousy — they are just beginners! But also the more ambitious a young writer is, the more experimentation they will do. Children who write nice stories — a bit like the latest book they've read, with butterflies in the margin — are possibly just trying to please their loving parents, not writing from the heart. Give them the freedom to make a mess of it!

**DON'T WORRY IF THEY DON'T FINISH THEIR STORY** Hounding children to always finish their work will make them hurry the story along to get it done and that will teach them very, very bad writing habits.

If they wanted to be a mechanic you wouldn't expect them to fix the car at their age, but just experiment with putting together model cars, so don't expect them to write a whole book either.

On the other hand, the story that they are writing could be a novel or a movie script. So let them just do lots of bits. One day, when they have time, they may finish a book — if they want to.

**PROVIDING THE TOOLS** Don't forget to provide your child with lots of paper or a word processor. It may sound obvious, but how many families have writing materials on hand? And when a child wants to write they want to do it now! Leave piles of scrap paper where they can be easily found and used whenever your child wants to.

Very active childre or children who have problems forming letters may look on writing stories as work, unless it's on a computer, and then it's 'play'.

**PRAISE** Who cares if it's a lousy story? It's their best. And there will be something there that you can pinpoint as commendable. So praise it and them and their hard work.

**BORROW BOOKS** You could borrow *How the Aliens from Alpha Centauri Invaded My Maths Class and Turned Me into a Writer and How You Can Be One Too*; it's a book designed to help children write. Reassure them that every writer has their own ways of making up a story. I outline my stories and think about them for ages before I start the actual process of writing by putting words on paper (or rather on screen!). But other authors find that boring — they'd rather just write and not know what happens next until they have written it!

In other words, give children help, but leave them free to do it their own way too or to find out which way works for them. And give children a great range of books so that they can absorb the techniques that other writers have used to say the things they want to express.

**DON'T SEND IT TO A PUBLISHER!** If the child is particularly proud of their work, don't send it to a publisher or to a writer asking how to get it published! You'll just be raising the child's hopes unrealistically. A book by a child gets published perhaps once a decade, if that. Children can write brilliant stuff — but it's usually only ninety-eight per cent brilliant. And that uncertain, amateurish two per cent will almost certainly make publishers reject the book and disappoint your child.

A child who wants to be a doctor doesn't expect to start practising at fourteen, and it's a really bad idea to let your child think that they might be a professional writer at fourteen too.

(The mum of Nobel Prize winner Patrick White paid for his early poems to be published, and in later years Patrick White did his best to get hold of every copy still in existence. The stuff you write at fourteen, even if you are brilliant, may be desperately embarrassing to you ten or twenty years on.)

On the other hand, a child's story can be a great gift for aunts, uncles and doting grandparents, and a great memory to hand on to their own children in twenty years or so. There are computer programs that will let you produce a reasonably professional-looking book. Or ask the advice of one of the companies that specialise in self-published books. Contact the writers' centre in your nearest capital city for a list.

★ ★ ★

# Chapter 4
# How to spot reading problems and how to help

# How to tell if a child has a reading problem

Does your child have a reading problem? Check through the list of indicators below.

- ★ They can't read as well as their friends or other children in their class, even though they seem as bright as the others. (Be especially concerned if a child who is doing badly at school has a really bright child as a friend. The child who is doing badly is almost certainly extremely bright too — but with a problem.)

- ★ They're frustrated by not being able to learn fast enough. (Okay, it's normal for every child at some stage to yell, 'No! No! I'll never learn my five-times table! My life is ruined!' But if this happens often there's either a learning problem or they're being pressured too hard to succeed.

- ★ They don't read as well as you think they should, even though they are keeping up with the rest of the class. (Be especially careful with this one. It's normal to feel that your child is a genius — but you don't necessarily need to worry that they are an underachieving genius if they don't get outstanding results. Hey, they just might be normal!)

★ They consistently reverse letters, especially 'b's and 'd's, even long after their initial introductory efforts. Ask a child to write the word *bed* or copy it from your writing to see if they can manage 'b' and 'd' yet. They may also write their words 'inside out' or back to front. Note, however, that a child can have major reading problems and not reverse their 'd's and 'b's! (A good way to teach which way 'b' and 'd' point is show children that the word 'bed' makes a 'bed-shaped' word.

★ They skip words or lines when they read or write.

★ Although they spell reasonably fluently, their spelling is inconsistent.

★ If they stare at a word or a simple drawing, the outline becomes fuzzy after ten seconds or less.

★ They don't seem to be listening in class.

★ They don't sit still in class — this includes not being able to hold a book still or repeatedly dropping it.

★ They have problems coordinating their hands and fingers when they write.

★ They daydream.

★ They have trouble estimating how long things will take. For example, they have no idea how much time has passed at lunchtime, and they are deeply involved in a long-term project when they should have left for school or been ready for the movies.

★ They move in a strange or jerky fashion.

★ They avoid writing or reading wherever possible.

If two or more of these indicators describe your child, they *may* have a learning problem.

But there may be — and usually will be — another cause.

The daydreaming child may be bored because they have already completed their work while other children are struggling; the wriggling child may simply be a very active child who gets bored or even physically uncomfortable sitting still.

And sometimes a child displays none of these indicators at all and is managing to read as well as the rest of the class, but they are still not reading as well as they might. *Often gifted children with reading problems are ignored because they are doing as well as most other children*. They can become increasingly bored and unruly, or quiet and withdrawn, depending on their personality and circumstances.

Children with reading problems only — as opposed to children who are slow at learning other tasks as well — are usually *more* intelligent than the average, not less. It's one of the tragedies for children with difficulties — they are children who'd probably love reading most but they have to struggle to learn.

I wish I could give you a magic formula to diagnose exactly why your child may not be reaching their full reading potential, but I can't. There are many reasons why a child may have problems reading — and each needs specialised diagnosis and treatment.

Don't be too impatient with a teacher if they fail to realise that little Percival really is a very bright child, who should be reading *War and Peace* by now. As a writer of children's books I get my share of parents showing me their child's 'brilliant' story and demanding I find a publisher for it. Out of about fifty parents a year who think their child is brilliant, perhaps, one is correct.

Teachers have no doubt become very, very wary of eager parents extolling their children's capabilities and wondering why they haven't won a Nobel prize yet. (It has to be the school's fault!) But on the other hand, as a parent, you do know if your child should be doing better and has a real problem. So don't give in. Keep pushing. But be tolerant of a teacher who has had a dozen parents with unrealistic expectations already this year and, of course, will lump you in with the rest.

Remember, too, that teachers want to teach your children well. Most teachers will be extraordinarily helpful and sympathetic, but it may take a while to convince some of them that the problem is real.

Don't blame them if your child has been in their class a while and has shown no improvement; children who have problems sometimes need to be taught differently from other children in the class, and teachers can't perform miracles. (Well, okay, sometimes they do, but you can't expect them as a matter of course, or blame the teacher when that doesn't happen.)

Often it isn't easy helping a child to read. It can't all be done in a normal classroom situation. But it *can* be done.

## Not so dumb afterall

Let me tell you a story. It's about a child — let's call him Jason — who as a baby showed all the signs of being a gifted child: talked non-stop from twelve-months onwards, asked questions like why didn't tractors have babies or how fast can God ride a bicycle, every 3.6 seconds. He asked and understood how electricity worked by the time he was three.

At four he decided to play the violin and zapped his way through the lessons. By seven his favourite bedtime story was *Lord of the Rings*. But Jason still hadn't learnt to read.

His parents weren't too worried at first — he was a bright child, he'd pick it up. There was no point pressuring him.

By the time he was eight he could write, as long as he copied words from the board. But each word took him twice as long as any other child in the class and even then his words looked peculiar — letters back to front, words inside out or even upside down.

The school still hadn't picked up that there was something wrong. All right, Jason was a little slow to read, but so are lots of children. The trouble with bright children is that they are very, very good at covering up what they can't do — and this child had a memory like an elephant. (Only, like my son, he still pronounced it *effelent*.)

But finally, after a lot of pestering, learning support reading was arranged at school — two lessons for an hour a week for six weeks, which was all the budget would allow. There were so many other children whose needs were greater.

Six weeks later there had been no improvement. By now Jason was convinced that he was dumb. Even the other children in the learning support reading class had been able to read at least a line or two by the end of the six weeks. But not Jason.

At this stage many parents, especially if they too had reading problems at school, might have given up and left it up to the school to do what it could.

Instead Jason's parents sent him to a reading recovery class. It was performing miracles for many children. Jason's parents crossed their fingers and hoped it would work miracles for him too.

Each afternoon Jason came home in tears. No, they weren't nasty to him. Yes, the other children were learning. But there was something about the lessons that deeply disturbed him. Some months later the teacher complained that Jason just wasn't able to concentrate and suggested medical intervention.

I'll gloss over the next four years. Other special education teachers, new methods, more failures. His parents tried every learning support system they could find.

At twelve Jason was surly, aggressive and very scared. He *knew* that he was dumb.

Then he was sent to a new, selective school. He failed the entrance exam, of course — he still couldn't write a logically sequential paragraph — but the school had the nous to see that something was wrong. They offered an oral exam instead. The boy who had failed the written test scored ninety-seven per cent.

The school accepted him on condition that he saw an educational psychologist who specialised in learning difficulties — and she was the one who picked up his problem.

Jason found focusing difficult. The special education reading classes he had attended, where they had tried to make him focus on short words or point at sentences, had been a nightmare for him. Jason was referred to an ophthalmologist. No, his particular focus problem couldn't be corrected (many can), but his learning difficulty could be.

Jason was taught to touch-type. It took three weeks. He was given a portable computer to do all his work on. When you touch-type you don't have to see what you are writing. You don't have to worry about focusing, you just write. Better still, the bright computer screen makes focusing easier, and Jason found that reading as he scrolled down the page was much easier for him than focusing on a single word.

Within six weeks he was reading and writing fluently. In another three months he had been put in the 'top set' class. His spelling was still appalling, he still wrote his words inside out, but not as often now, as typing can be much faster than writing longhand and for some reason Jason found it easier to write quickly than slowly.

He still had to learn punctuation and how to write an essay, and all the other literacy skills his friends had learnt. He still got poor marks because of this, but now his teachers realised that he was a bright child with problems.

By fifteen his marks were good. He had extra coaching for his literacy problems. He was now able to read and write so confidently that he no longer had to use his computer. Even his handwriting was approaching normal.

But he still *knew* he was dumb. Even in his last two years at school, when his grades were excellent, he knew that he was dumb. He sat for his leaving certificate but planned to emigrate with an assumed name when he failed, so that no one would know.

He didn't fail. He was in the top twenty in the state in three subjects, and his marks were good enough for any of the courses that he might choose. He cried when he got his results and his parents cried too; it had been a long journey.

Scars don't heal easily however. All through his first year at university he waited to fail again. He still thought that somehow he was there by fluke, that everyone would find out how dumb he really was. He's doing his PhD in chemistry now. Don't ask me exactly what he's doing — I don't understand — but Jason does.

He's a voracious reader too — mostly thrillers, but occasionally the odd 'deeper' book that he loves and cherishes. He wrote a letter to me last Christmas. (His parents had written to me years before to ask for help — they'd heard that I was dyslexic too — and Jason and I have corresponded at odd times since.) He wrote in longhand, not on the computer. I doubt that anyone reading it — even someone whose spelling is much better than mine — would have dreamt that this child had ever found reading or writing difficult. But it so easily might have turned out differently . . .

---

★ ★ ★

# Seeking professional help

So many children never learn to read or write comfortably. They slip through the system.

One of the most frustrating things for anyone with a dyslexic child is that so many experts have their own pet theory about what causes dyslexia and how to overcome it. I have lost count of the number of times I have been told, 'Oh, X is absolutely wonderful! He/she can teach *any* child to read in one ... or six ... or twenty ... easy lessons,' by giving them coloured glasses, or training their eyes to do such and such, or slowing down their focus.

And, yes, usually these techniques are effective — although often not quite as magical as claimed — but NOT necessarily for *all* children, as I know all too well. There is no one technique that solves all problems. I wish there was. As a family we have tried everything we could find on offer for various family members with problems, and although most techniques helped each particular child a little, no one single technique or reading course worked by itself.

There is no one thing that is dyslexia — it is many things. Dyslexia is used as a convenient label for someone who has reading and/or writing difficulties — and there are a myriad of reasons why this can be so.

Any special education tutoring *may* help if your child has reading problems, as it teaches children to focus and work out their own problems as they spend more time on the subject. Feeling as though someone cares enough to help doesn't do any harm either.

Sometimes too, a learning support teacher speaking slowly and clearly in a quiet room, without distractions, may alone be enough to help children recognise how words are made up of sounds, especially if they come from a family where words are slurred or the TV is always making distracting noises in the background.

Many boys, in particular, process sounds more slowly than girls, and this may be part of the reason that more boys than girls have reading problems. Simply training teachers — or parents — to speak more slowly and distinctly may have a dramatic and positive effect on these boys' ability to learn these skills.

To be really effective you need to know *why* a child is having problems before you can work out the best way to help them.

## Obtaining the right diagnosis

It is often very difficult to work out *why* a child is having problems. Children who are slow at learning to read are usually lumped together. Even though there are different reasons for their problems, the same techniques are often used for everyone.

A child who has problems focusing, for example, will

need different help from one who is simply a slow learner. One boy I know was given pages of large text, few words and lots of white space in his special education class for years. This just made him feel even more of a failure, as he couldn't even read a 'baby book'.

He had the same form of dyslexia as I do — we find it difficult to focus on single words and have to read quickly to read at all. I find the standard learning-support text agonising to read — it's really disorienting for me to try to focus on it. And reading with a finger pointing along the line makes it even worse! (I *can* focus; I just must do it *quickly*.)

Sometimes, too, children are diagnosed with problems like Attention Deficit Disorder (ADD) without thorough investigation. ADD does exist, but so do misdiagnoses. I've known children who are much brighter than the other members of their class (and so are bored and daydreaming) and children who are of a 'let's conquer the universe before breakfast' nature — very active children — to be all lumped together in the ADD basket.

This is not the teacher's fault. Teachers almost invariably have far too little time to perform miracles. Even a special education teacher may not be able to diagnose certain problems, although they may be pretty good at working out which experts the child needs to consult to get a proper diagnosis.

**WHAT TO DO** Children with reading problems *may* need a specialised diagnosis by one of the following specialists:
★ an opthamologist who specialises in reading problems
★ an audiologist
★ a speech therapist

- an occupational therapist
- a nutritionist
- a neurologist
- an educational psychologist
- a psychiatrist
- a consultative peadiatrician who can assess any sleep or other health problems.

Some children may need to see more than one of these; others may not need to see any. But many reading difficulties *will* need an expert diagnosis, and in other cases, rare conditions like brain tumours still need to be ruled out.

## Accessing a specialist if a problem exists

The gut feelings of parents are pretty reliable. If you suspect a serious problem, be persistent!

Your family doctor or your child's teacher may well be reassuring, and say 'they'll grow out of it' or that 'they are within normal limits for their age', or 'let's just wait and see'. Trust your instincts!

Insist on specialist help now. The longer problems are left the harder it is for children to catch up, and the bigger the scars they'll have from thinking that they are dumb.

Sometimes children may need more than one specialist and I don't want to promise miracles, but sometimes a few months with the right specialist can make it seem as though a miracle has occurred.

**CONSULTING THE CLASS TEACHER** The first professional to consult is your child's teacher. Teachers see children with others of their age and can often judge whether a child has problems, or is just young for their age. This can be a delicate balancing act for teachers; many parents become offended when a teacher says that their child has a learning difficulty.

It is possible that your child may just be having problems in one area of learning, and the teacher can give them extra work to do at home so that they can catch up. The teacher can also refer the child to the school's special education teacher (assuming the school has one).

**CONSULTING THE SPECIAL EDUCATION TEACHER** A special education teacher may be able to recognise a child with special needs and coordinate the appropriate referral. They should be familiar with specialists who liaise with the school and work with other professionals to provide appropriate support for your child at school.

All being well, the special education teacher will work out which specialist the child needs, liaise with the specialist and parents to help coordinate any treatment, and help the child catch up with their schoolwork.

If the school does not have a special education teacher, ask your family doctor for a recommendation or contact SPELD (Specific Learning Difficulties). This organisation can provide specialist advice in an enormous range of areas, including the recommendation of psychologists and specialist tutoring, computer programs, reading material etc. Look in the phone book for your local branch.

**AN EDUCATIONAL PSYCHOLOGIST** An educational psychologist can assess a child's intellectual functioning and educational attainment, and obtain an overview of their auditory and visual skills. A psychologist's report will also be necessary for older children if they need to ask for extra time for examinations (and other allowances in Year 12), and it may also help in convincing the school to let the child use a laptop in class, or to provide other assistance such as a special education teacher to work with them.

Not all psychologists will continue to work with your child. Most will just give you an assessment of whether there is a problem or not. Some may refer you to other specialists who can design a program of assistance; others may leave this up to you. In other words, a psychologist may be able to tell you if there is a problem, but may not be able to offer solutions about what to do about it. This varies from psychologist to psychologist, and some do specialise in learning difficulties and will be able to give a lot more help.

**AN OPTOMETRIST** An optometrist will check your child's eyesight and recommend glasses if necessary. You don't need a doctor's referral to go to an optometrist — you'll find a list of them in the phone book. But your child may not need glasses; they may have other problems that can be diagnosed by a behavioural optometrist.

**A BEHAVIOURAL OPTOMETRIST** A behavioural optometrist will investigate what your child's eyes do. Children with reading difficulties often have problems with convergence and tracking, and the behavioural optometrist can discover if this is the case, and will also give you ways to overcome the problem.

**AN AUDIOLOGIST** Audiologists check to see that the child can hear. Some audiologists have additional specialist training in following what the brain does with what it hears. They can check for auditory processing disorders.

**AN OCCUPATIONAL THERAPIST** Occupational therapists assess and work with children who have coordination, concentration, handwriting or other sensory problems. Sometimes children diagnosed with Attention Deficit Disorder (ADD) have never learnt how to concentrate, and can be taught.

**A SPEECH AND LANGUAGE PATHOLOGIST** These specialists will investigate your child's strengths and weaknesses when using language. They'll be able to work out a program to help improve skills like visual sequencing, memory and sound awareness.

They'll also give ongoing therapy (tutoring) and counselling. Most speech and language patholigists work in close connection with schools and other professionals.

**PAEDIATRICIAN** Sometimes medical problems make it difficult for children to learn. They could have anything from a gluten allergy to a snoring problem. You will probably suspect that something is wrong already, if it is a health problem rather than a learning one, but if you are concerned ask your doctor for a referral to a paediatrician.

**PSYCHIATRIST** Some children have emotional issues that need to be resolved. Others may be suffering from depression or panic attacks. You will need a referral from a doctor for a psychiatrist. Ask your doctor's advice. You could also ask the special education teacher or a paediatrician — anyone regularly involved with children with problems to recommend a psychiatrist who relates well to children.

It's important to make sure that the psychiatrist is experienced working with children and their problems, relates well to your child (in particular) and to everyone else involved in helping them. If that isn't happening, go to another.

Psychiatrists do specialise in various problems — and you will probably need one with real experience in this area. But sometimes, too, one with no particular focus on children's problems can develop a great working relationship with a child — be prepared to try another if the first one is unsuccessful!

**TUTORS** You might also like to enlist the assistance of a home tutor to help your child catch up on work missed at school.

Many tutors advertise in the phone book; some are associated with various methods; others will work on their own.

Make sure that the tutor is not just a teacher earning extra money, and certainly not just a university or high school student. Working with children with learning difficulties is not classroom teaching at a slower pace. The person *must have* additional training and experience.

It's important, too, that the child feels happy with the tutor, and really feels that they are getting somewhere. If after two visits your child still doesn't like the tutor, or feels what they are doing is 'silly', find another tutor. Persisting with one that doesn't suit your child may just make them even more discouraged.

★ ★ ★

# Specific problems

Many causes of reading problems aren't learning problems at all. Go through the following checklist, but remember that children can have more than one problem.

- ★ Did your child walk and/or talk at a later age than their peers?
- ★ Do they have problems understanding abstract concepts?
- ★ Do they prefer to spend time with much younger children?
- ★ Do they have a health problem that slows down their learning?

Children who are slow learners will probably learn to read with the same methods as most other children; they will just take longer to do it and may need more individual attention with fewer distractions. Even then they may never reach the same standard as other children their age — although on the other hand you may be surprised how well they can do with extra help.

Make sure that your child is getting all the help possible from their school, but also see the suggestions in Chapters 1 to 3. No matter how much help children get at school, they'll do best if they can get help at home too.

Your child could also be exposed to a range of social or physical problems that can interfere with learning — from the obvious (a broken arm, glandular fever) to problems at home or at school. The following are just some of the possible causes of a child's problems.

## Vision and focus

Some children have problems seeing words and letters, or making sense of what they see.

This can be simple short-sightedness, easily treated and diagnosed by an optometrist, but there are other conditions that limit a child's ability to focus or coordinate what they see. These must be diagnosed by an ophthalmologist who specialises in these problems.

Eyesight and focusing problems are possibly some of the most commonly misdiagnosed causes of reading problems. Some common ones are listed below.

* Some children have problems reading in certain lighting conditions or can focus better wearing prescribed coloured lenses.

* If your child turns their head as they read a page or loses their place, they may have problems coordinating their eye movements.

* If your child can only see a few letters at a time, they may have a small visual span. They, therefore, have to keep looking back to check what letters they have read.

★ Some children have problems focusing for longer than a few seconds. After that things blur. (These children will probably hate it if you point to words as you read.)

★ Some children can see well but can't process what they've seen — they find it difficult to distinguish between shapes or colours, or can't remember what they've seen. This is partly inherited, and partly learnt. All children have to learn how to remember what they've seen and put the pieces together to make sense of it — for example, they put together mouth, nose and eyes and say, 'Hey, that's Mum!'

**WHAT TO DO** If your preschool child isn't as good as other children at making things out of blocks or Lego or joining the dots, or your older child keeps misreading words like *cat* for *cut* or leaves the ends off words or misreads *69* or *96*, ask your family doctor for a referral to an optometrist or opthamologist who specialises in developmental problems. You will definitely need a specialist. Don't think that because a general optometrist has checked your child's eyes that they are okay. The optometrist needs to be experienced in visual perception tests and visual motor coordination tests (although they may use different names for these) and be able to give you a report on what the problems are and how they can be helped.

You may find that the optometrist works with an occupational therapist, or refers clients to one for help correcting their problems. Children don't have to be short-sighted to have problems.

You can try having your child taught touch-typing. That way they don't have to focus on what they are writing and as they type, they will become familiar with words and find reading easier.

You can also teach your children how to focus and use their visual memory. Like any skill, the more you do it the better you get — and the earlier you become skilled the better. Ask them to practise 'seeing' what they did yesterday. Then ask them where they were or what Egbert was wearing or what flavour their ice cream was. Or play memory games. Put an object on the table — say an apple — then ask your child to shut their eyes and remember what it is. When they open their eyes again, you put a banana next to the apple, and ask them to shut their eyes and say 'a banana and an apple'.

Or put twenty things on the table and give the child a minute to look at them. Then they shut their eyes and remember as many things as they can. You should participate in these games too, to show that they're fun, not lessons.

Another good game is 'This Way Round'. On squares of cardboard draw people (or horses, fish, dogs etc.) looking to the left. Then draw one person or animal looking to the right. Your child has to choose which one is looking to the right. Or play card games like Snap or Old Maid or play dominoes.

## Hearing

Most children have trouble hearing at some stage because of wax in their ears or after a cold or other illness. While this is temporary, it can still interfere with learning to speak and use words. Other children may lose some of their ability to hear from illness, or it may be inherited.

Children as young as two months old can be tested for deafness. But as a child gets older, you can pick up clues.

Does your child:
* watch your face carefully when you are talking to them, or turn their head to one side?
* have trouble talking or understanding when the TV is on?
* confuse the beginning or ends of words?
* not like playing with children not familiar to them? (Bear in mind that the reason for this may be many and varied.)

If you suspect that your child has hearing problems, talk to your doctor at once. Early diagnosis and treatment as well as learning support will make an enormous difference!

Some children are not really deaf but do have some trouble isolating the sounds that they want to hear (or that you want them to hear) from competing sounds.

Does your child:
* confuse similar sounding words like *pat* and *pot* or *big* and *bag*?
* have problems with rhyming words?
* mispronounce *lots* of words?

Some children are just slower than others at learning to discriminate between sounds. It doesn't mean that they are dumb or slow generally — just slower in that area of learning. Others may have a hearing problem.

**WHAT TO DO** Ask your family doctor for a referral to an ear, nose and throat specialist, and an audiologist.

If your child doesn't have a hearing problem, make sure that you speak clearly and distinctly to your children. It's difficult for a child to work out how to spell *cat* for example, if the word they've mostly heard is just *ca* or *at*.

And make clear hearing easier! This means turning off the TV, radio or hi-fi system and asking other members of the family (and this includes adults) not to play computer games while the child is attempting to read or listen, learning to spell or taking a dictation.

## Discriminating between sounds

Discriminating between sounds is also a learned skill — one that can be taught. Take time to listen to different sounds with your child. The following are some useful games you can play with your child. None of these strategies will be an instant solution — but slowly and surely they will make a great difference.

**SITTING AND LISTENING** You can play this game in the car, at the beach, anywhere that there are different sounds to listen to.

Mum: What can you hear, Emma?
(Emma shrugs.)
Mum: I can hear a car. What sound does a car make, Emma?
Emma: Vroom!
Mum: Can you hear a truck too? It's a different sound. Can you hear it?

**RHYMING GAMES** Adults should take the initiative with this game, but later children will probably choose to join in.

Dad: I see a car. Ha, ha, ha, I see a car. I see a dog, no it's not a frog, it's a dog, dog, dog. I see a cat, it's very fat.

You don't have to do this so often that you sound demented, just now and then. Children like rhymes and rhyme games and will work hard at joining in. You can also try making up sentences using as many words that start with the same sound as possible: *King cat caught a carrot.* When children can make up sentences like this themselves, try finding words that end in the same sound: runn*ing*, jump*ing*, fish*ing*; b*at*, f*at*, c*at*, m*at*, s*at*.

**COPYING 'FACE SOUNDS'** You go 'oo', and exaggerate the shape your lips make to produce the sound. Then have your child make the same sound, moving their lips in the same way. Do a few new sounds every day.

## Memory and recall

Children also need to develop the ability to recall and remember things. And again, some children are slower than others. There are a number of strategies you can use to teach children how to remember.

#### REPEATING WHAT THEY ARE TOLD

Mum: Go and get your raincoat. Now, what did I ask you to do?

Jason: Go and get my raincoat.

Mum: Okay, now think it inside your head instead of saying it. Can you do that?

Jason nods.

Mum: Good boy!

#### IMAGINING WHAT THEY ARE TOLD

Dad: If I have to remember something, I try to imagine it in my head. If Mum says, 'Will you take out the garbage please,' I make a picture in my mind of me carrying the rubbish bin. How about you try it? If I say, 'Get your raincoat please,' what will you do?

Jason: Imagine me and my raincoat.
Dad: That's good! Now, are you doing that?
Jason nods.

**MEMORY GAMES** Play 'I Packed My Bag and I Took ...'.
Each person in turn has to add an imaginary item to an imaginary bag and remember all other items added by other family members.

Dad: I packed my bag and I took ... a banana.
Mum: I packed my bag and I took a banana and an apple.
Emma: I packed my bag and I took a banana and an apple and a fruit popper!
And so on!

This is a great game to help teach children how to remember things, especially if you say: 'Imagine each one in the bag,' or 'Try to link each one in some way: a banana is bigger than an apple and an apple is smaller than a fruit popper ...'.

## Coordination

Is your child clumsy? Unable to coordinate their writing, catch balls or ride a bicycle? There can be many reasons for coordination problems, from eyesight problems to brain injury at birth or acquired, muscular dystrophy, motor neurone disease, epilepsy, multiple sclerosis, including less likely ones such as a brain tumour, thyroid problems, diabetes or hyperglycaemia. All of these will have other symptoms too, but it is worth having any coordination problem checked out by a professional.

**WHAT TO DO** Have a chat with your family doctor. Make a list of all possible symptoms before your visit — often one symptom alone may not strike a chord, but several together will suggest what the problem may be.

Encourage your child to play a sport or do an activity that teaches coordination. My son got over his right–left coordination difficulty with an enthusiastic karate teacher who made him do repeated left–right exercises with hands and feet. At the end of three years of weekly practice he was fine. I've seen clumsy teenage girls blossom and no longer worry exactly where to put their hands and feet after they have been exposed to a few months of jazz ballet. Ballet, dancing, ice-skating, swimming, any ball game and many other activities all teach hand–eye coordination and how to use and move your body, as well as being fun and keeping children fit.

There are also less obvious activities that children who are less physically adept or not at all competitive often enjoy — such as ball-against-the-wall games, jacks or knuckles, skipping games, juggling, stilt-walking and other circus skills. All these are still wonderful approaches for developing different levels of fine and gross motor coordination. So if your child loathes rugby or hockey or whatever, there are still plenty of other avenues to explore. See the games in Chapter 1 for more ideas.

Show your child how to touch-type. It's far easier to learn to read and write if you don't have to worry about making your fingers form the letters. And typing will help children *look* at the words and think about them, so they will learn to read faster too. Don't worry, they *will* learn handwriting because children like to be like everyone else.

## Eating problems

Is your child eating well enough, or could they be diabetic or hyperglycaemic? As any parent who's been to a birthday party knows, sugar highs exist. Some children who eat junk food, especially lots of sweet food with no protein or complex carbohydrates to balance it, may well have problems concentrating.

Children who are diabetic or hyperglycaemic may also have problems concentrating.

**WHAT TO DO** If your family has a history of diabetes or hyperglycaemia and you suspect that your child has problems, ask your family doctor to give your child a glucose tolerance test. And if you are unsure what your child should be eating for their best development — or have a child who is a picky eater, who demands junk food or has developed other bad eating habits — ask your doctor for a referral to a nutritionist. They'll not only be able to say what your child should be eating, they'll help with strategies to make sure they do.

Food can often become a power battle between parent and child. If your child has a limited range of things they will eat, start working on the problem. (A few cookbooks with bright pictures of healthy foods are a great start — get your children to participate in choosing and cooking the recipe you'll cook next.)

The exceptions to this commonsense approach are anorexia (which needs immediate diagnosis and treatment if you suspect it), bulimia (literally starving and gorging, it also needs professional help at once) and vegetarianism, which is a legitimate moral stand that children may decide to make.

(It may also be a way of asserting their individuality too — but that isn't a bad thing either.)

Vegetarianism, however, is no excuse for not eating well (even if the family cooks may have to discover a few more sources of protein and iron), and there are plenty of books that give advice. Hunt them down in the local library.

Too often, children hate eating fruit and vegetables because no one has ever tried to make them attractive. Many children are intimidated by a whole large apple, but will eat a plate of sliced fruit.

## Lack of sleep

While this is mostly a problem for adults, children can have sleep problems too and a lack of sleep will mean that the child can't pay attention properly at school.

**WHAT TO DO** If your child wakes often during the night, snores, coughs, is extremely restless or just doesn't sleep their regular nine hours, have a chat with your family doctor, who may refer you to a sleep clinic.

## Family issues

It's difficult to concentrate on anything — let alone something as new and complex as learning to read — if you're stressed or worried.

Sometimes children can seem quite happy with changes at home — a new brother or sister, a parent now living away from home, the illness of someone they love, a grandparent moving in — but their schoolwork is suddenly affected.

**WHAT TO DO** Have patience and don't stress about their temporary slowness. With any luck they'll catch up.

Concentrate on being loving and reassuring: let them talk, give them lots of cuddles and a reliably regular routine. And if problems look like continuing for a while, arrange for them to talk to a counsellor, either a private one or the school counsellor. It's often a good idea to have a chat with the school counsellor anyway if there are problems at home, just so they can alert the teachers to be especially tolerant and supportive.

It's also a good idea to encourage children to talk to trustworthy friends and relatives. Find the child a mentor figure outside the immediate family, not necessarily to help with their problems, but to give them encouragement and a feeling that they are appreciated. The mentor can be a relative or anyone with standing in the community (from a football coach to a writer), who is prepared to spend time with the child or even write to them regularly and reassure them that they're worthwhile.

Encourage your child to write about their problems in a diary, or write stories and essays or draw, sculpt or paint. These are all good ways to express pain and distress and put them into a form that doesn't hurt so much.

Provide refuges in the form of books, videos or DVDs. Make sure that it is happy, relaxing, escapist stuff — because children do need to escape!

You can also encourage them to join a relaxation exercise class or do yoga or meditation or take up power walking or aerobics for a natural high and also to help them sleep soundly — anything from exhausting exercise to bushwalking and dancing.

And as for the reading problems, try the steps to reading given in Chapter 3. But don't pressure them. Offer help, but tell them they're wonderful too!

## When I'm stressed ...

- ★ I talk about it with family or friends.
- ★ I go for a walk in the bush — or at least somewhere with trees or water.
- ★ I imagine a wombat munching in our garden (especially when I'm at the dentist) or that I'm floating almost under the water in our swimming hole.
- ★ I imagine I have a monkey's tail that's growing from the end of my spine down, down to the ground then through the earth until it curls around the centre of the planet — that's a good one just before I have to speak in front of an audience!
- ★ I get to work solving the problem. Activity is much less stressful than doing nothing and worrying. Even if I'm just as far from a solution, actually *doing* something makes me feel better.

### Noise and disruption

Sometimes, even with the best intentions in the world, home is going to be chaotic, especially if both parents are working or a member of the family is ill or there are long-term visitors or lots of children or ... You can probably add a hundred more things.

Is there a quiet place where children can read? Is your child given time to 'turn off' and read quietly without other demands from family, friends or other organised activities? Are they given half an hour 'downtime' to read in bed or at least look at pictures in a comic book? If not, you might want to consider how to improve your child's environment.

**WHAT TO DO** Provide a quiet place in the house — one room where children can read or do homework without any distractions and interruptions from the TV or other children. (I used to read in our family dunny — it was the only quiet place around! Then I made myself a 'room' under the back stairs. Sometimes a parent's bedroom can be designated 'the quiet room' for reading or studying.)

If this isn't possible, at least give children a quiet corner — and provide earplugs! (They cost a few dollars at the chemist). I'm serious — children are often expected to read or do homework in conditions I couldn't work in!

And please, please, please, please — turn off the TV! Constant background noise makes it harder to think, work and concentrate.

## School

If a child hates school they probably won't learn well there.

Bullying is, sadly, the most common school problem. However, there can be other problems: the (luckily rare) teacher who takes out their own grievances on the children; a 'best friend' who has home problems that are making their friends worry too; the child who has become involved with a crowd of children with their own problems and who rebel at learning anything. Sometimes children just feel that they've been in trouble too many times and now feel that they have been labelled a 'troublemaker' and can't escape.

Sometimes one child or a small group of disruptive children can disturb the learning of the whole class.

Unfortunately a growing problem in city schools is noise — I was at a (very expensive private) school not long ago where teaching had to be halted every seven minutes as an aircraft flew over. Other schools can be disrupted by traffic or building noise.

For some children a less formal style of teaching and learning can also be a problem; the noise and movement around them are extraordinarily disruptive. These children can be helped immensely if you can find a rather traditional school where the children are fairly quiet and remain seated, and there is only one activity going on in the classroom at any one time.

Some children — and adults — can tolerate noisy places. Others find it incredibly difficult to concentrate. (I'm one — I become stressed if there is any loud noise at all around me.)

**WHAT DO TO** Try to find out what the problem is. If you can't and just have a tearful child who says they hate school, consult their teacher, the school counsellor (especially if bullying is the problem — children can be helped to learn to cope with bullies) and, if necessary, the principal.

## Attention disorders

Attention Deficit Disorder (ADD) and Attention Deficit Hyperactive Disorder (ADHD) do exist. Yes, some children are wrongly diagnosed as having ADD, but others are dramatically helped by either the medication or learning support specifically tailored for ADD children.

The trouble is that you can't take a blood test and discover that a child has ADD. Doctors diagnose ADD because of the way the child behaves — they're impulsive, inattentive or hyperactive, with a poor short-term memory. And there can be many other reasons why the child has all of those symptoms: they may be very bright and very bored; they may be a naturally active child; they may be so deeply upset by a school or home problem that they can't concentrate; or they may have a hearing, visual or some other problem which diminishes their concentration skills.

Not all ADD children are hyperactive, although they're the ones that you mostly notice. Some ADD children can be quiet and withdrawn and daydream a lot, but still have poor short-term memory, are impulsive and have difficulty concentrating. Other children can learn to concentrate with the help of an occupational therapist — and for these children medication is not the long-term solution.

Doctors and, to some extent, counsellors and teachers only see children under a limited range of conditions. Parents, however, need to work out if their child has problems under *all* situations. For example, if a child is just having trouble concentrating at school, it may be that they are bored, or are being bullied, or have a specific learning difficulty. If the child is bright it may mean that they are bored, and so will fidget or be disruptive.

Does your child act first and think later? (Of course they do. They're children!) But do they do it more than other children their age?

Do they have trouble remembering that you asked them to get their jumper two minutes ago? (Yes, of course they will if they're preoccupied by cartoons or a mate's visit. But again do they do it more than other children their age?)

Do they have problems concentrating? This is really the key question. Very active children may seem to have problems concentrating because they'd rather be out doing things! But when they are doing things — painting the garden furniture twenty-seven colours, playing a sport that needs concentration, building the most magnificent sandcastle on the beach — they can concentrate wonderfully (children with Asperger's syndrome do this).

Children with other learning difficulties may not be able to concentrate enough to read, but they will concentrate on a long complex story that's being read to them until the reader loses their voice.

Children with ADD have concentration and memory problems in *most* situations — not just some of them.

**WHAT TO DO** Have your child diagnosed by a doctor who specialises in this area. Provide the doctor with as much information as you can to help their diagnosis, but try to be even-handed — academic parents who have a child who would rather be zipping around a football field than reading and who loves comic books instead of *The Wind in the Willows* can so easily think that their child has a problem. They don't — they're just different from you.

Work out a wide-ranging treatment regime with the doctor — not just medication. Children with ADD will need help with learning skills like organisation and concentration; even if the medication is successful, it won't solve all the problems. They will need help from an occupational therapist. Medication alone is never enough.

A child with ADD may also need to be assessed and treated for hearing or visual problems — speech therapy and occupational therapy may help here too. And both children and parents may find counselling helps them cope with the problems that ADD can cause.

Also, take a look at 'Fast processors' in Chapter 5. These children are sometimes misdiagnosed as ADD. They concentrate so well that they need to zap through things to find more stimulation, and they can be bored with children their age and therefore don't mix well. But these children do concentrate well at home, and here the assessment of a child by both parents and teachers is crucial — the parents know what the child is like when they are happy and interested, the teachers know how well they are performing compared to other children.

# Chapter 5
# All children learn differently

# How we learn

There's no such thing as 'the average child'. Children have widely different interests and temperaments, and each child has their own unique way of learning. Sometimes children don't have a 'reading problem' — it's a teaching problem because that child may learn best in a particular way. But all children will benefit if you can work out the learning style that suits them best.

## Children learn differently

No two humans process information in exactly the same way. And we don't learn to read in the same way either.

Perhaps the best example of this is when my husband, Bryan, and I are watching a movie. Bryan is a visual processor; I'm a verbal one. Bryan loves diagrams; I get lost in car parks. I zap out half a dozen books a year, while he takes three days to write a letter. He can understand a wiring or software diagram in the blink of an eye. I find that a map of a shopping centre blurs in front of my eyes.

So when we watch a movie together I miss all the visual clues and Bryan misses the verbal ones. Bryan is always saying, 'Hey, did you see that?' and I say, 'No'; and he can never understand how I can follow what's going on if I dash out to the kitchen to put the kettle on — as long as I can hear what's going on, I'm fine.

In school Bryan learnt what was written on the board; he probably missed half of what the teacher said, but if it was written he was fine. I mostly daydreamed out the window, but as long as the teacher kept on talking, I still followed what was going on.

Humans learn in various ways:
* visually
* verbally
* physically (kinetically)
* from our sense of touch and smell
* from interactions with other people.

And probably many other ways as well!

Most of us process information using a combination of these various ways; others are very strongly slanted towards one means of information processing over all the others.

## Spatial or visual learners

These children are often intellectually gifted and that is a problem, because their intelligence masks the *real* problem and that problem can mask their intelligence, so they get frustrated.

A visual learner needs to see things, not hear things. They need things written down. Phonics are easy for children with a high verbal IQ, but they are harder for visual learners to grasp and may be very difficult indeed for children who have perceptual difficulties or who are 'speed' learners.

To see if your child is a predominantly visual learner check the following list:

- ★ They are much brighter than their schoolwork results suggest. (Although this is the case for children with other problems too.)
- ★ They have a very vivid imagination.
- ★ They often have vivid and disturbing dreams.
- ★ They are often very distracted by things happening out the window or at the back of the class.
- ★ They can have more difficulty with times-tables and spelling than written work, although if those tables and spelling lists are made visually interesting with graphics and colour this can help.
- ★ They can be very disorganised.
- ★ They often love computers, graphics, TV, doodles and music.
- ★ They are often extremely good at problem solving.
- ★ They are very creative and excellent at analysis.
- ★ They are far more sensitive to noise, distractions, light, colour and the sheer intensity of sensual experience than other children.
- ★ Often they forget their homework or what they are supposed to be doing in class; they wander off task.
- ★ When spoken information is given to these children it's almost as though it's another language — they pick up bits of it but not enough to make sense.

**WHAT TO DO** If your child is a visual learner, you should teach them to read by having them concentrate on the sight method where they learn to recognise whole words, as well as phonics. Yes, they'll still need some phonics, but using flashcards and reading books over and over with the child looking over your shoulder until they recognise the words and the way they fall into patterns will probably teach them more.

Follow the steps to teach children how to read in Chapter 3 but use a computer as much as possible to teach that child at every stage, so that they can *see* all the steps written down. You write something then they write it after you.

Let them do as much homework as possible on computer too.

## Auditory learners

These are children who learn best from things they hear, not things they see. These children may hate diagrams and find it difficult to focus on written words. They probably misread assessment questions or homework instructions and in severe cases can't retain a visual image in their minds. They may show no interest in computer games, jigsaws, Meccano or anything you have to look at to solve. They'll often like talking a lot, analysing people and their motives and, in the beginning anyway, do far better at oral work than written work.

(In extreme cases these children — and adults — can't retain the image of what a word looks like in their mind for long enough to learn it. But this is very rare.)

Ask the child to look at a word, letter or black and white simple sketch. If it blurs within ten seconds, they have a problem focusing and will have learnt to gather information about the world mostly from what they hear, not from what they see. (I can only look at a word for a fraction of a second before it blurs.)

**WHAT TO DO** Work out *why* they are having problems focusing on things. It may just be something they are born with, but it may also be a symptom of an eye problem or another illness). Have your child examined by your family doctor and ask whether they think the problem needs to be investigated further. If necessary, ask for a referral to an ophthamologist who specialises in focusing problems. They may also need exercises to help them coordinate and focus and 'track' across the page.

It may be useful to have them taught touch-typing, so they don't have to look at what they write. Once they are familiar with written letters and words, it is far easier for them to learn to read.

Help children learn to focus on words so that they learn what they look like. Have them trace over the words with a finger or a pencil or copy text from a page onto a word processor while they say the word at the same time. They only need do this a few times until they know what the words look like.

The hints below for 'fast processors' also apply, in the main, to auditory processors.

## Fast processors

This is the form of dyslexia I have, and it seems to be one of the most common forms of learning difficulty.

How do you recognise us?
* We speak quickly, and tend to gabble.
* Spelling and reading are poor, although once reading is learnt we are fast, often fanatical readers.

- ★ We invert words or even swap words in sentences, and have problems with the letters 'b' and 'd', although this is not particularly important as many children with this problem can manage these letters quite well.
- ★ We're good at analysis; we can often make far-flung connections and we learn best when connections are there to be made, rather than just lists of information.
- ★ We're messy.
- ★ We can not only do two things at once — even carry on two conversations at once — but delight in doing so.
- ★ We try to do *everything*, rushing from one project to the next passion. As a school report said of one child: 'George will never regret the things he has never tried to do …'
- ★ We have poor coordination, especially left–right, but it's also bad in dancing, athletics etc.
- ★ We have problems focusing. I can only read a line of text if I do it *fast*, otherwise it all blurs.

Fast processors have to process information quickly or they don't process at all.

Some children with this problem can learn to read before they go to school by the word recognition method, but many others don't.

These children tend to be much brighter than average. For this reason they may also be disruptive as they're bored. Their confidence is easily destroyed too. These children *know* that they are brighter than their friends, yet they can't manage even the simplest schoolwork their friends fly through.

**WHAT TO DO** *Don't* give these children the standard reading coaching text — large words and only a few on the page.

This makes the problem worse, because children can't focus on large words. They need *lots* of text on a page, or comic strips which have few words but lots of images to focus on. And *don't* point to each word as they read, this makes everything much worse for them. They need to be able to see everything at a glance, so trying to slow down their focus makes it almost impossible for them.

Teach these children touch-typing, and then teach them to use the computer. Teaching a fast processor touch-typing is possibly the single most important thing you can do for them. Some fast processors, however, might have difficulty with coordination aspects (we're not all exactly the same) but if it does seem to work I'd suggest not bothering with reading until they can write, and don't bother with correcting spelling until they are confident typists. Computers go fast, so children with this problem will be able to both read and write fast too. And the faster they can go, the easier it will be for them.

Typing requires a different kind of coordination from that used when you are writing a word. Many fast processors find that because they only have to concentrate on one thing at a time — they don't have to focus, or form their letters, which are both problems — it's easier to type than write.

Children with major coordination problems will still find typing difficult, but this is something an occupational therapist can help with. And children with disabilities can be given specially designed keyboards. But for most children — and certainly for most fast processors — typing instead of writing can be a miracle solution.

Once they can read and write fluently using a computer, teach them calligraphy. You'll often find that once they have mastered literacy, they'll go back to doing 'what everyone else does' anyway.

Remember that reading problems are not always clear cut. Don't push the computer solution if it clearly isn't working — some children will need a lot of help just to be able to learn to type. And some children may never write easily, even with a computer, although they will learn to read fluently.

Give them advanced reading material straightaway. It's not easier for these children to read simple texts — in fact it's more difficult, as the words are usually spread out. But on the other hand comics — especially sophisticated *Phantom*-type ones that adults also like — are great for these children. There is a lot of picture activity on each page, even if only a small amount of text.

Once they have mastered writing and reading, give them regular extra coaching if possible to catch up on all the sentence construction, punctuation etc. that they have missed.

They will still need to learn to spell. Without spelling tutoring, they won't learn to spell, and will find it difficult to distinguish words they haven't seen before.

Don't get them to use a computer spellchecker as they work — it'll just interrupt their flow — but do encourage them to use it afterwards and to do their own editing.

## Active children

The active child is the one who always seems to be wriggling around. He develops ants in his pants if you try to get him to concentrate on a page (and yes, he's usually a boy). He would rather be galloping across the plains or conquering the universe than sitting still!

There are many reasons why a child may seem to be 'hyperactive' — so active that they just can't concentrate on things. See if your child does any of the following:

★ They may be kinetic learners — children who learn best when they are moving about.
★ They may just notice more of what's happening around them — like visual processors — and so be more easily distracted.
★ They may be bored in class because what's going on *appears* boring to them.
★ They may be a fast processor — a child who processes information so fast that they are easily bored.
★ They may be being bullied at school and are too stressed to concentrate. Stress can manifest itself as restless, pointless (to the observer) activity, rather like the displacement activity that captive animals sometimes display.
★ They may be stressed by family or other problems.
★ They may have an attention disorder — ADD or ADHD.

I suspect that the most common reason why some children, especially boys, can't sit still long enough to learn is just that they are physical little creatures who like moving about.

**WHAT TO DO** Make sure that these children have plenty of physical activity, before and after school.

It may look regimented and old-fashioned, but callisthenics, physical exercise or any form of organised aerobic activity makes an enormous difference to many children, especially nowadays when so few of them walk or ride bikes to school.

Check that your child isn't with a mob of friends who just 'hang out' at lunchtime instead of doing something active. Encourage them to do something physical for at least part of the time.

Enrol children in organised activities like karate, dancing or bushwalking — whatever suits them best. If possible, encourage them to walk to school or to the bus stop, or ride their bicycle. But most importantly, remember that your child doesn't have to sit still to learn to read and write.

## Kinetic learners

Very active children may be kinetic learners — they learn better by *doing* things. Even if they are just an easily bored child, they'll concentrate better if they can move while they learn.

**WHAT TO DO** Find a nice blank concrete wall outside. Buy pump-action water pistols — the really big kind. Get your child to form their letters and write their words with their water pistols on the walls. (I bet they'll still be there writing when it's time for bed.)

Give them small water pistols filled with water-based paint, and have them write words with water pistols on butcher's paper — bathing costumes and an outside venue are a must for this!

Play a 'Run and Chant' game. Make them run once around the garden chanting the spelling of one word. When they get back they have to write it down. Once they manage that, they get another word and another run.

Try any of the following:

- ★ Give them cardboard with words written on it and some Blu-Tac. They have to move around the house attaching them to the appropriate item and then have to take them off.
- ★ Make plasticine letters and then make words with them.
- ★ Write in sand — but not enormous letters as then they wouldn't be able to focus on the words. Letters about 30 centimetres high should be big enough to be fun but not too large to cause focusing problems.
- ★ Write with a torch while they spell out various words. Get them to jump as they say each letter.

Encourage your child to learn good physical crafts like weaving, cooking, gardening, woodworking etc. but give them books and articles about it too, so that they learn the theory as well as the practice. This also goes for any sport they love; show them that there is a theoretical as well as practical side to any sport, with information available on everything from training methods and diet to the lives of sporting heroes.

Do a mural or a learning wall during each school term in the family room. Stick butcher's paper on a wall and every day get your child to add something they've learnt, such as new spelling words, labelled drawings or even just drawings. Add the times-table, a map of explorers' journeys — whatever's relevant. Writing up what children have learnt is a good way to really fix the information in their mind — and again they are up and doing something, instead of just sitting and watching TV.

Many active children will find touch-typing a wonderful option. They will be able to work *fast*. Show them how to link onto their favourite Internet sites too — sport sites, science or movie sites.

Most importantly, keep them at it! Active children have so much else that preoccupies them that they easily forget what they've learnt yesterday. Regular short sessions every day until they read fluently are essential.

**BOOKS FOR ACTIVE CHILDREN AND KINETIC LEARNERS** Give active children books that can be read quickly. Comics are often best for really active children, ones with lots of adventures like *The Phantom* or *Footrot Flats* that they can read quickly for fun and dash off to play again.

I wish that all libraries had a stack of comics for children. It's not that I want children to read comics instead of books, but a comic can be a great learning aid, to give children fluency and make them realise that reading is actually fun. Each picture in a comic gives the child clues about what the text is about, and the short snappy text is very easy to focus on too. Most children *love* comics, and they can really get reluctant readers going.

Once they have been beguiled by the short snappy comic book format move on to the longer story-length comics like the *Asterix* and *Tin Tin* series, loved by so many boys (especially those with a bent towards history or geography).

## Easily distracted children

It's often difficult to tell whether a child has a genuine reading problem or ADD or is very active. And some children have never learnt to concentrate for any length of time.

**WHAT TO DO** If you suspect that your child *does* have ADD or ADHD, ask your family doctor for a referral to a specialist or seek an appointment with an occupational therapist who specialises in children who have concentration problems.

There may be other reasons — emotional, nutritional or some other undiagnosed medical problem. Children who have hearing or sight problems often seem easily distracted because they are unable to see or hear well enough to concentrate.

Ask yourself as well, whether your child *really* is easily distracted or just very active. A very active child will concentrate for extended periods on the things that interest them. An easily distracted child finds it difficult to settle on anything for long.

If your child is just an active child, go with the flow! Count your blessings that your child is energetic and healthy and may also be extremely bright. A real passion for getting into things and inquisitiveness are often signs of high intelligence.

Turn off the TV and try to provide your child with quiet spaces and quiet times. You should also try to set a good example by giving yourself some quiet time too. If you're always flustered and jumping from one disaster to another, your child will learn to do the same.

★ ★ ★

Teach your children to be organised. It's something they will thank you for later. Have them make lists of things to be done, make a schedule for each day of the week on a whiteboard in their room or in the kitchen, sort clothes into categories, sort rubbish for recycling and place it in the correct bins. Children respond well to an ordered life where they know what is going to happen and when.

Teach children how to concentrate. This is something that children have to learn; it doesn't come naturally. Often children who can't concentrate simply haven't been taught how to. You can read them long, complex but fascinating stories, like *Harry Potter* or *Lord of the Rings*. Or tell them long interesting stories about when you or their grandparents were young so that they get used to listening for longer periods of time.

Try turning off the TV at mealtimes and have long conversations instead. They will learn that one remark can lead to another and then to a discussion where they have to think and put their thoughts in order and into the best words possible.

Discuss social, political and moral issues with your children, so that they learn to think, focus and argue. There should be no yelling. 'But I want it *now*! Everyone else has one!' is not an argument, it's a demand. An argument is a reasoned discussion, and it doesn't have to get heated, although it may if people feel passionate about a position. (It's important for children to know that they can put a case and be heard and also that other people can state their position and some things will remain unresolved to be thought about and returned to later.) But children do need to practise thinking things out; help them to get their thoughts out into the open.

You can also encourage children to do projects or craftwork. Let them choose something they are interested in. (Take them to the non-fiction section of the library and fossick around for good suggestions.) This will teach them that long projects can be fun, and that the more work you put into something, the more fascinating it becomes.

Teach children how to work on lengthy tasks — how to plan what they are going to do, get the right materials, do the job, finish the job and clean up afterwards. A good practice job is repainting garden furniture or the garden fence. Let them choose the colours. A friend and her children wall-papered their toilet with two-hundred pages filled with children's drawings, poems, jokes, times-tables and favourite pictures cut out from magazines. It took most of one set of school holidays and each summer holiday to redo it. It is the most fascinating loo I know.

## Non-fiction children

These are usually boys. My favourite story about a child like this is a friend of my son's — let's call him Paul.

At the age of twelve, according to his teacher and the reading coach his parents had hired, Paul was unable to read more than a few words and his writing wasn't much better. He would stare out the window, he wouldn't concentrate on the subject at hand and reading just seemed beyond him.

Paul was a farming child. His parents had a large mixed farm, but Paul's real passion was chooks. He and my son were trying to cross Australorps with Auracanas to produce a chook that regularly laid large blue eggs (but I won't go into that).

One day when Paul was at our place I received a veterinary textbook on chook diseases in the mail; we are talking large book here, tiny text, a real textbook, but it did have good photos. So I gave it to Paul, thinking he'd like to leaf through it.

He clasped it to his chest, sat down with it and four hours later was still reading it. He muttered, 'I haven't quite finished it yet,' when his mum came to pick him up, so I let him borrow it. He left with it still clasped to his chest. Three days later he rang me to say he'd finished it but could he read it again. Actually, I don't think I ever did get it back.

Paul just didn't like fiction — especially the type of fiction so often given to problem readers. And no one had thought to give him stuff he was interested in. Paul discovered farming magazines: *Australian Poultry* magazine and a horde of books on the topic he was interested in. And he kept on reading, although not, I have to say, in school. (He left at the earliest legal date, but is doing extremely well anyway.)

**WHAT TO DO** Offer your child non-fiction books that provide information about 'real' people and things, not 'pretend' ones. There are great books for children like Anthony Hill's *Soldier Boy*, that are true stories and will make a non-fiction child understand that they are reading about the real world, not chick books with horses and people discussing their feelings.

Try giving your child magazines about their favourite subject, or a range of magazines on different topics so that they can find out which subjects they're interested in. It doesn't matter if these are adult magazines — if they are interested, they'll work it out. Or try reading half of an article to them so that they know what it's about, then let them read the rest. They'll now know what the difficult words are likely to be, from V8-engine and foul-brood disease of bees to estuarine species of fish.

Find websites about interesting subjects and show them how to browse. Then let them find stuff they like. (Okay, you may need to include a bit of censorship here.) Undirected browsing is a surprisingly good way for children to pick up reading skills.

You can give them a newspaper every day and read a few items with them — if the child just isn't interested in current affairs they might enjoy articles in the motoring, sports or fashion sections. You could also encourage them to read out bits from newspapers or magazines to you (maybe when you are preparing the evening meal). This enables you to gauge what is interesting to them, allows them to feel that they are contributing to your education and often gives you both fertile ground for discussion. It is also a lovely companionable way to spend twenty minutes together.

Give children recipe books — the ones with great colour pictures of each dish — and let them work out what they want for dinner. (You'll be amazed how many children will ponder all the ingredients to make sure that it doesn't contain coconut or pumpkin or whatever they particularly hate. The reward, of course, is that they get to choose what's for dinner the next day).

As a rule non-fiction children often do far better with adult reading material as they often don't like 'kids stuff'. For many boys, military histories and biographies are a fabulous source of reading material, and once they are reading eagerly and fluently, it's amazing how they can be tempted by some types of fiction as well.

Don't worry if a child chooses something that you consider to be too complicated or sophisticated. Most children practise a form of censorship of their own, glossing over the bits that make no sense to them yet and concentrating on the bits that do make sense. And don't worry too much about unsuitable adult material either — people process words differently to pictures, especially moving images. Censor what your child is allowed to watch on film or television, but let them read whatever they want to. (I'm talking about books here — not *Big and Bouncy* or other adult magazines with pictures.)

A child allowed to read *All Quiet on the Western Front* will not be spooked by gruesome images in the same way that one who watches a violent film will be. They will be haunted by big questions about violence and war and the randomness of history and how people's lives are changed by other people's decisions, but these are quite appropriate questions to be haunted by.

And as for 'big words', as long as they can understand eight words in ten, they'll pick it up — especially if they feel comfortable asking you to tell them what the really hard words are.

## Emotionally talented children and social learners

These are children who simply find other people more important and fascinating than schoolwork. They'll want to fit in with their friends; not show anyone up or seem brighter or more able than the rest of the class and they simply won't be enormously *interested* in excelling.

**WHAT TO DO** These children should be gently pushed towards group projects, group research and projects and subjects about *people*.

Let them know early about the caring professions, from social work, medicine, speech therapy and music therapy to teaching. Convince them that they'll need to do reasonably well at school if they want to get into these important and rewarding areas. Find them books about people helping people or doing things together or about animals.

Make reading a social event for your child and get them to read with their best friend. Best friends are often more intuitive teachers too, as they have more experience of a friend's needs and more recent experiences of how they learnt that technique. (I learnt algebra from my best friend in five minutes, after hours of formal teaching had failed.) Ask them to help younger children, encourage them to join or form a club — a horse club, a fan club, anything that involves being social and using their reading and writing.

These children would also enjoy writing a small magazine or newsletter with and for their friends on subjects that interest them — whether it is fashion or fishing, music or motors.

## Slow Learners

These children aren't just slow at learning to read and write. They are slower to learn all sorts of things.

The emphasis here, however, is on 'slower'. These children will learn to read, write and whatever else they need to learn, but it will take them more time — and if that time isn't given to them right at the beginning, they will get further and further behind. With these children it's not so much a matter of how to teach them — it's finding the extra time and human resources to do it.

Adults often severely underestimate 'slow learners'. I remember my first public reading of one of my stories. The third group to come in were children with an intellectual disability and I thought, 'Hey, this is impossible, I wrote this story for extra bright children!'

I've never had such a wonderful audience. I had to speak much more slowly, it's true, and keep pausing. But they laughed in all the right places and at one point, where a child in the story says that adults often agree with you because they don't really listen to you, some of the audience literally fell off their seats laughing and gave pointed looks towards their carers.

These children were slow learners — but they got every point the other children got, and more. Give these children time and they'll get there.

**WHAT TO DO** Slow learners often benefit from some of the suggestions for very active children too, as their attention span may be limited.

But mostly reassure slow learners that they *will* get there in the end. The worst thing you can do for a child is convince them that they are dumb and that there is no hope.

On that note, we once had a man classified as having an intellectual disability work here for a week. Yes, he was slow at understanding things and he was a very slow reader. But he was also fascinated by the wildlife here and — slowly — made his way through a heap of CSIRO scientific reports on wallabies, platypus and habitat destruction.

Above all, do give slow learners good and challenging books once they *do* learn to read, and in the meantime read to them — their favourite books, books about things that interest them.

## Slow language developers

These are usually boys — and sometimes boys with a loving older sister or caring parent who makes it easy for them to live comfortably without talking much. (If you ever hear one of your children — or yourself — say, 'Little Percival would love a slice of cake, please,' instead of letting little Percival ask himself, take a closer look at little Percival's language development in case he has problems that you — with the best will in the world — have been perpetuating.

Children who are slow at learning and using language will probably be slower at learning to read. They may also have problems learning to hear the sounds that make up individual words. You can tell if your child is a slow language developer by checking the list below.

* They are slower to learn individual words than other children their age.
* They are slower to speak in sentences.
* They're not having conversations by the time they are three.
* They play silently with other children or, more likely, have a range of noises — the roar of a truck, the whir of a flying plane — that they use instead. They may also let the other child 'tell the story' of the game they are playing, while they concentrate on the action.

On the other hand, they are no slower at learning to walk, catch balls, play happily with children their own age or a bit older or understand what's going on around them. They are generally as bright — or even much brighter — than most children.

**WHAT TO DO** Say words very, very clearly when children are learning to read. They may be slower at learning to pick out individual sounds. And try to speak clearly and distinctly as much as you can without going totally barmy with the effort.

You should also play 'Making Word Sounds' from Chapter 1 regularly — in the car or walking to school.

Help your child through each stage of learning to read with the techniques outlined in Chapter 3. Ask for advice from your child's teacher and learning support teacher. And please, be patient and don't panic. Yes, learning to speak early and using enough words to stump a professor of English *is* a sign of high intelligence, but a child can be a slow language developer and still be brilliant. They are slower, but they will catch up and even overtake their peers in language ability.

Seek help the minute you suspect that your child is taking longer than other children to talk fluently. Take your child to a speech therapist. Okay, they may just be slow, but there may also be another problem that needs treating. The speech therapist can also help your child catch up with their peers.

## Mabel's story

I came across Mabel a couple of years ago. She had no particular education herself — left school at twelve, married at seventeen — but for years she had been volunteering at the local school to help children with reading problems — and she had the most extraordinary success rate. People spoke of her as though she had magic in her fingertips.

Her secret? Mabel has a naturally clear, distinct voice and she spoke slowly and deliberately. All those children who were having problems simply hearing how words were made up had no problems at all when they tried to write or read the words Mabel articulated. And she had enormous patience, tolerance and love, and children felt cherished rather than shoved into a group of dummies. Sometimes you just get a miracle like Mabel.

PS: I suspect that after thirty years Mabel also had the experience to know when to suggest a visit to the doctor or other specialist.

---

## Bright but bored children

This is a child who is often misdiagnosed with ADD or ADHD, but instead of finding it difficult to concentrate, they concentrate extremely well and so have often finished their work long before other children, or they are too bored to begin in the first place. So they stare out the window or daydream, if you're lucky, and disrupt the class if you're not.

If you suspect that your child may be 'bright but bored', ask yourself the following questions:

★ Did they walk or talk earlier than their peers? Many gifted children don't do this. (One extremely bright young man I know didn't talk until he was three.) But early verbal ability especially is often a sign of a gifted child.
★ Do they ask so many questions that you feel like hiding under the bed to get some peace?
★ Do they seem to learn things faster than other children their age?
★ Are they creative — make up stories, songs, music, drawings that show originality?
★ Are they forever curious and enthusiastic?

* Are they always into things?
* Do they have a memory like an elephant?
* Are they intuitive — think on many levels, rather than from 'a' to 'b'? Children who just seem to pluck questions or answers out of thin air are really taking in all sorts of information and decoding and interpreting. (My step-grandson, for example, asked me how bees made honey. After the explanation, he asked, 'But how do they make the jars?' He was taking what he had been told and adding to it what he knew already, he went one step further.)
* Do they have a wide range of interests. (Leonardo da Vinci was interested in just about every aspect of art and science.) Gifted people are usually fascinated by more than one area and often these interests appear far apart — music and mathematics, for example, bushwalking and engineering. An early interest in lots of things is a sign of a gifted child.

**WHAT TO DO** Children who poke their fingers into sofas, who ask one hundred and forty-six questions before breakfast, who always want to *do* things and need at least four adults to keep them amused and occupied can give a saint a breakdown in twenty minutes. But all these are also signs of highly intelligent children who process information quickly and are hungry for more.

The sooner these children learn to read and find the books they enjoy and need, or learn how to manipulate computers, circuit boards or any other activity that they'll finding challenging and absorbing and open-ended (the more they do, the more they'll find *to* do) the better for everyone's sanity.

You may think that a gifted child will never have a reading problem, but this isn't the case. Sometimes these children are just so bored that they don't pay any attention at all.

Gifted children may also be fast processors and have great trouble doing things slowly. Even if your child isn't a fast processor, many of the hints given earlier for these children will be useful for a gifted child.

## Children who have just missed out

This is possibly the most common reason why children have temporary reading problems; they have missed out on a step or two somewhere, either because they were away from school, or were stressed about something for a while, or had a teacher that they didn't get on with, or a disruptive child sitting next to them. There are hundreds of reasons why children may just have missed out on a vital stage in learning to read, and then just keep getting further and further behind.

These children don't need an underlying problem solved; they just need a bit of help to get them on the right track.

**WHAT TO DO** Possibly nothing — they'll probably catch up anyway — but it'll be better for their confidence and happiness if they can be helped. Make sure that you ask about learning support at school — at this stage almost any extra help may be enough to get them on the right track.

Go through the reading steps in Chapter 3 to see where the problem is and then work on that area at home. Tell the teacher where your child is having problems so that they can help them catch up.

★ ★ ★

## Chapter 6
# Encouraging a reading culture

# Little by little ...

You want to encourage a 'culture' of reading so give children a book to 'read' while they are watching TV or a DVD, so that they don't associate reading with 'let's just be quiet and well behaved' times. But do have quiet learning and reading times, so that children learn how to sit and concentrate.

Don't force children to sit and read if they are bored. If they're bored they either need to be learning something that isn't boring, or the reading activity has gone on too long. Young children especially have short attention spans but quiet learning, with no TV and no distractions, will teach them *how* to concentrate.

Show your child how much you love reading too. Talk about the great book you're reading, so that they know about this great grown-up activity they are going to learn one day. Let your child *see* you read and enjoy a book. Say, 'I'll be there in two seconds — I just have to finish this page!'

★ ★ ★

# Secret adult's business — reading together at home

It's really important to show children that reading is fun — not just something that is good for them. That is really why adults read books — because we love them, a sort of secret adult's business that children can join in once they learn the rules.

A long time ago there were public readings — people with well-trained voices and a dramatic manner would read stories to a whole hall of people. I suppose that the book readings on ABC radio are the same thing in different clothes.

It's possible for the whole family to enjoy reading books together aloud, just as they sit around the TV together. (I bet that in ten years time you can't remember a single evening spent around the TV, but you'll remember the reading together with love and happiness — and possibly a few retrospective giggles too.)

Given that you'll get so much pleasure from family reading, it seems a bit mean to add that there will be literacy advantages too — not just the reading practice children get, but the feeling for them that reading is something to enjoy, not work at, and that it's something that people they love and admire enjoy as well. They'll also get an ego boost from knowing that you are both enjoying the same sort of book, instead of them reading kids stuff and you reading a grown-up book.

Family reading is especially valuable to the child who is having problems with reading, too, because it *is* fun stuff. For less confident readers:

* Choose a favourite book that you have read to them at least once before, so that they know in advance what the difficult words (like *volcano* or *wizard*) are.
* Try reading alternate pages or even paragraphs with them. (You should go first.) This will give them most of the words that they may find in the next page or paragraph and make the challenge much easier.
* Write down a story that they tell you one night and then get them to read it to you the next night. Or you read it to them the second night and they read it to you the third night. This is even more of an ego boost, as you can tell them it's such a stunning story that you can't wait to hear it again and, as by now they will know it almost by heart, it will make reading it aloud far easier.

If they are terrified of reading aloud, however, don't ask them to. You read aloud to them while they do their chores and wait until you think they may be confident enough for you to say, 'How about you finish this chapter while I stack the dishwasher?'

## What and when to read together

**PLAYS AND OTHER PLEASURES** When I was a child, my mother and I used to read plays together — she'd take some parts and I'd take others and it was a lot of fun. It was also very easy reading. Mostly I'd only have to read a line or so at a time and because Mum was reading the same book too, she mostly read out the difficult words before I had to work out what they were.

Not all children like reading plays aloud — especially some boys may find it almost as embarrassing as kissing their mums goodbye in public. But some children can find it a real joy.

By the time I was ten I was writing plays for my younger brothers and sisters. (Their favourite was *Headless Hound*, a puppet show about a headless dog; well, he had to be headless — my baby brother had pulled his head off and eaten it.)

As well as giving children reading practice, reading plays aloud can encourage them to put on performances for you and any other adult who can be tempted to take a seat. It'll give them confidence to talk in public, and help them learn to speak clearly and with expression. But most of all, it will be something that they can do themselves (or with you, their brother and sister or their friends) and feel proud of.

**READING TO ENTERTAIN THE WORKERS** Take it in turns to read or do the washing up, or read aloud and tidy the room. One person works, the other person reads to entertain them and then you change places.

Choose books that everyone will love for this — funny books or short stories or crazy poems like Roald Dahl's hilarious retelling of fairy tales. As always *Lord of the Rings* is a great standby — you'll get years of housework done to *Lord of the Rings*!

And remember, even a reluctant reader may be less reluctant to read aloud if it means someone else does the tidying.

**FAMILY POEMS** Children tend to love poetry — the rhythm of it and the song in the words. Children as young as four have fun finding rhymes for words and putting rhymes together — and rhymes are a superb way for children to unconsciously absorb how words are put together.

Make it a family habit to write a poem for everyone on their birthday, or to write a special Christmas poem about what the year has been like. They don't have to be long complex poems — a limerick is fine:

*There once was a child called Brett*
*Who rode on his bike for a bet ...*

Or if their name is Samantha or Bartholomew or something else that's hard to find a rhyme for:

*It's Samantha's birthday today*
*And so I would just like to say ...*

And of course the poems can be a lot ruder, and if children are doing them they probably will be; they can even put them to music to embarrass their brothers or sisters in forty years' time.

But basically it's fun and it's making children feel at ease playing with words, and giving them confidence that words are theirs to use — and this confidence will stand them in good stead when the poems and songs are cherished memories.

By the way, I was at an eightieth birthday party last year, and the children — now middle-aged — all read out some of the ruder birthday poems they'd written for their brothers and sisters fifty-odd years earlier.

It was happy and hilarious and by the end of the afternoon their own grandchildren were scribbling down poems to be read in fifty years' time!

**LOO POEMS** A friend's loo is papered with family poems, limericks and jokes, plus the odd reminder too: 'You know who: don't forget to wash your hands. No — wet hands aren't the same as clean hands. You have been *warned*! love, Mum.'

There's a family rule that you can only paste over someone's poem after it's been there for six months, then it's fair go. Luckily there's a surprising amount of wall space in a loo, especially now that Tim can reach the ceiling on a stepladder. It's the most interesting loo I know.

If you live in a rented house, hang butcher's paper from the ceiling and stick poems to that.

**OTHER POEMS** Poetry — the sort that rhymes, has rhythm and preferably tells a story — is often easy reading for children. The short lines and the rhymes help them predict what the next word will be.

Look for simple poems to begin with, like Roald Dahl's *Revolting Rhymes*. Once children are reading fluently however, you may find that they love other poems — as a very young child I loved poems like 'The Lady of Shallott' or

'The Forsaken Merman' or 'The Man from Snowy River' — poems that told stories. Or ones like 'Break, Break, Break', that I loved just for the sound of the words and the bright images they gave me.

Many poems are also short; you can read most of them in the time it takes to stack a dishwasher and you get a heck of a lot of beauty or meaning per second — very time-effective for active children.

Like all books, you'll need to match the poem to the child, and encourage them to taste different kinds of poems too. But for most humans a good poem is a rich experience. It's a bit like a piece of passionfruit sponge cake with cream and fresh strawberries from great-grandma — you don't want too much, but the delight and the memory stay with you for years.

**CAR BOOKS** I get carsick if I read in a car and so do most children. But car trips provide a great opportunity for children to listen to tapes of talking books or CDs. You can take them out on loan from the local library. Or make your own tapes — everyone in the family can take turns reading part of a story — it's fun waiting to hear your turn come on.

**READING WHEN YOU'RE SICK** Most sick people need cosseting — a feeling that they are being loved and looked after. I don't know anything as cherishing as being read to, no matter what your age. And if the book is *Green Eggs and Ham* and you are forty-five and the reader is six and needs help with the big words, so much the better!

Encourage children to read to anyone who's feeling sick (assuming it's not desperately infectious or the invalid needs sleep more than entertainment). Children need training in how to show compassion too.

**DIARIES** A few rare children keep diaries most of their lives. Most keep diaries on and off — and get great pleasure reading them years later.

Diaries, of course, give children reading and writing practice, as well as preserving not just memories, but also a record of, 'Good grief, did I ever feel like that?'

Encourage children to keep diaries but don't pressure them to do so. But a small decorative book is a great way to tempt children to keep a diary just for their holidays or over Christmas or the first weeks of a new school year. Explain that they'll find the diary a fascinating record of their own history when they are older.

# Getting children hooked on books

Okay, first the good news: there is a magic potion that will turn bored children into contented munchkins, help them perform better at school and make them generally happier and eager for life.

It's called reading.

Now the bad news: there isn't any fairy dust you can sprinkle on books to make them the sort each child will love! It takes work to teach children that reading is fun.

Children will always associate reading with hard work because it *is*, especially when you have only just learnt to read and it is very hard to find the books you like.

### All children are different
This is probably the hardest step for any loving parent, especially ones who love books and reading. You have to accept that children are almost always different from their

parents, and that the books loved by one generation tend to differ from the adored books of another generation.

My son, for example, has a steady diet of books where one man single-handedly overcomes everything that stands in his way. He hates books where people *talk* about things — exactly the sort of book I love. (Boys mostly prefer male main characters. Girls are more tolerant.)

If I'd tried to stuff my son with the books I adore, he'd probably hate reading. Listen to children and find out what sort of books they love ... and don't shudder if they want yet another space adventure or book about horses.

## Get going to the library

Libraries are free, warm in winter and cool in summer. They nearly always have a children's corner with lovely books all displayed on low shelves where children can look at and reach for them.

Borrow as many books as the library rules allow — you choose one, and then let the children choose the rest. Read one there and take the others home. Most libraries have a weekly story-telling time for children and some community centres do too. Hunt them out. They not only get children hooked on books early, but will also get children used to library spaces — any new space can be a bit intimidating for anyone who isn't used to it.

If your child falls in love with a book, buy it if you can — or just keep borrowing it. A deeply loved book will probably be loved forever — and passed on to the next generation.

## Don't underestimate children

If a child doesn't like reading it's tempting to give them short, snappy books. And children may read them, but it won't get them hooked on books. The books that hook you ar the ones that you love. Often children are bored because they are only given simple books, or books which do not stretch their reading capabilities or inspire their imagination.

Find half a dozen good solid stories at the library for your child to choose from adventure books to 'chicks' books' with characters and emotions. You need real meat on the hook if you're going to catch a child. And be sneaky — read half stories or chapters. This will tempt them to read the other half to see what happens.

If you have absolutely no idea what books your child might like, have a chat with the librarian at your nearest large library or the teacher-librarian at your child's school.

You can usually tell if a child loves a book: they will literally hold it close to their chest as they walk with it — not to mention eat over it and take it to bed with them. The books you love are the ones you remember years later or all your life.

A funny book can also be a *great* book, like those by Morris Gleitzman or Terry Patchett's *The Amazing Maurice and His Educated Rodents*. This is an hilarious book with lots of widdling jokes, but it's also a rich and fascinating book that will wriggle down into children's minds.

The most sought-after books today, the Harry Potter books, are rich in characters and events and they're *big* too — the sort of book to lose yourself in.

## Help children read widely

I love cherries and chocolate, but I'd hate to have to live on them, even if they did provide the entire range of nutritional needs. And it is the same with books. It's a real mistake to think that children will only love one sort of book — that a boy who loves raunchy and fast-paced adventures won't equally love a deeper more complex book at some other time.

Children need to be taught that just as different foods suit different times, so different books suit different moods. When you're feeling braindead after a heavy day at school, you may like something light and funny. When you're bored on holidays, you might like something deeper that involves you emotionally and makes you think.

Children also need to be told that they may not like what their best friend likes, whether it's *Harry Potter* or anchovies on their pizza. And even if they don't like what most of the rest of the class like, the world is full of an extraordinary range of books, and the books they will love are out there somewhere.

## Sam's story

I met Sam with his dad at a writing workshop I was giving. Sam was enthusiastic all through the workshop, bouncing up and down as we all outlined a story together. (It was about a tribe of hippy elephant surfers living on an island on the Great Barrier Reef who were having trouble with the vampire mermaids.)

Sam seemed like exactly the sort of child who devours books at one sitting then demands his parents give him another one *now*. But his father informed me gloomily afterwards that Sam hated reading.

'Does he have trouble reading?' I asked. Sam had certainly seemed very bright and imaginative for his age, and often it's these children who do have problems learning to read.

'No,' said Sam's dad. 'He can read very well. He just doesn't like books.' Sam nodded next to him.

'Maybe he just can't find the sort of books he likes,' I suggested.

Sam's dad got a bit indignant at that. 'His mother and I adore reading! The whole house is filled with books.'

'But are they the sort Sam likes?' I asked.

'There are all sorts of books there! He can choose whatever he likes! I've still got all the books I loved as a child and so does his mother. We must have every children's classic ever written. *The Lion, the Witch and the Wardrobe*, *The Wind in the Willows* . . .' He was getting quite heated by now. Sam just looked bored.

'Do you have, *The Day My Bum Went Psycho*?' I asked.

Sam's head jerked up and a light of fiendish joy appeared in his eyes.

'Sam wouldn't like rubbish like that,' his father declared.

The light began to go out of Sam's eyes.

I wish I could give you a happy ending for this one: how I gave Sam's dad a list of ten books and bet him a hundred dollars that Sam would love every one of them and when I won the bet we spent them all on the sort of books Sam loved, not the ones his dad thought he should love. But it didn't happen like that. Sam's dad walked off in a huff and Sam trailed after him.

Different children like different books. And children who are given the wrong books — even with the very best of intentions — may turn into reluctant readers, even though their reading skills are pretty high level.

---

## How to help children find fabulous books

Children need to be taught how to find the books they'll love. Books have to be hunted out — and just like our ancestors had to learn how to hunt a sabre-toothed tiger, it takes time to learn to hunt for books in shops and libraries and how to select the books that they like just by skimming the back cover, the first page and a bit of the middle.

Here are some useful suggestions that will hopefully steer your child towards being an enthusiastic reader demanding more books now — and *why* aren't you supplying them?

**TEACHING CHILDREN TO ASK** Encourage children to ask their teachers, the school librarian or bookshop sales assistants, what are the most popular children's books at the moment, and then try them.

Tell them to ask their best mates. After all this is the way most adults find out about good books — we tend to read books recommended by friends. Do reassure children that just because they don't like the same books as their best mates, they may still love books.

On the other hand, your child may share similar interests with other children — horses, football etc. — so get them to ask if they have read any good books about their passion.

Also encourage your child to tell their friends when they find a cool book (or, even better, a series that goes on for several books) so that they can share their enjoyment and sense of discovery with their friends and, hopefully, create a sense of excitement around the notion of books and reading.

**LETTING CHILDREN KNOW THAT THEY CAN STOP READING** Encourage children to borrow as many books as possible each time they go to the library, but if they don't like a particular book after a chapter and a half, encourage them to stop reading and try another. Take them back to the library pronto if none of them are worth the effort of ploughing through.

Forcing a child to read a book that bores them is one of the best ways I know to make children hate reading. Yes, children need to be introduced to their heritage of great literature, but there is a heck of a lot of great literature in the world, and some of it will be the stuff your child will like.

**TEACHING CHILDREN TO 'TASTE' BOOKS!** This is possibly the most valuable literacy skill of all. No, you can't judge a book by its cover, but covers can still be a help in working out if you are likely to like the book or not. The blurb on the back of the book is also helpful.

Encourage your child to leaf through the book and look at the style of writing: does the writer use a voice — boring, blokey, twee, jokey, romantic etc. that turns you off?

Read a paragraph from three separate pages. This will probably be enough to let you know if the book has an even chance of keeping you turning the pages.

Most adults have already learnt this technique — but it's a great help if someone else teaches it to you early.

**KEEPING A LIST OF GOOD BOOKS** I tend to discover an author then go through a lovely time reading absolutely everything they've written. All libraries and bookstores have a computer database of books an author has written and whether they are available.

Libraries can order books in from other libraries — this is called an inter-library loan. All bookshops can also order a book in for you if the publisher is still selling it. If not, contact a good secondhand bookstore and they'll hunt round and find it for you — usually for less money than it would cost new, unless it is a very old or rare edition. And of course you can also order books through the Internet.

**ENCOURAGING CHILDREN TO TRY NEW BOOKS** Let them choose their full quota of books at the library and choose a couple of books for them on your quota. Read them bits of it to tempt them. Don't push. If they're interested, they'll say so. Children are rarely masochists and won't deprive themselves of something they like. Nor will they carry on listening to or reading something they hate. Remember the aim of the exercise is to find the books your child likes, not get them to appreciate the books that you love.

**PUTTING UP A SUGGESTION BOX** Ask if you can put up a suggestion box at your local library, so that all library members can ask for books they'd love to see in the library. Then teach your child to look at book review pages, bestseller lists, children's magazines, children's websites and the websites of their favourite author to find out what new books are coming out that they may love — then bung a suggestion into the box fast!

**LOOKING FOR SECONDHAND BOOKS** Show children how to browse through the shelves of secondhand bookshops or at secondhand book stalls at markets. Thrift shops, garage sales and fetes are another good source.

**STARTING A BOOK-SWAP CLUB** Ask your school to start a book-swap club — one day a month children bring in books they'd like to swap. Every child can bring one book in and take one book out. (The book has to be in good condition.)

★ ★ ★

# Book groups for younger readers

Adults like reading groups — a meeting to talk about a book, eat sticky buns and chat. Children love them even more. A book group is a party, but a party with a purpose — the sort of party you remember long after any memory of jumping castles has faded.

## Book groups for littlies

How to do it: Parents meet once a week or once a fortnight with their children. Each parent brings a book to read and a plate of something to eat and each adult takes it in turn to read a book to the assorted children while the other adults chat and stop little Mikey from eating Jessica's stuffed rabbit.

The group can meet either at each house in turn or at a library or anywhere that will donate space and perhaps a tea urn. (Libraries are great as you can use their books for the day and then borrow some to take home.)

Result: Children get exposure to lots of books; they

learn that stories are fun even if they're not sitting on mum or dad's lap; and they learn that other children like books too. And if it's at the library, they learn that book-filled places are fun places to be.

And, of course, in between reading books the children get to play and eat stuff, and the adults get to socialise.

Little children love to participate when you read to them. If the book has a rabbit in it, make them rabbit ears or give them pink rabbit noses and whiskers with face-painting pens and have them hop around in a circle before and after reading the book. If the book talks about a big elephant and a small ant, show them how to make big and little gestures.

## Reading groups for early readers

This is great for weekend afternoons or school holidays. It works with between two and ten parents.

Each week (or fortnight or day for that matter — if it's a long boring holiday) choose who will bring the book. It's best if it's a book that none of the children have read. Again, bring a few buns, plates of fruit, drinks etc. to make it a party as well.

The adults take it in turns to read a chapter of the book. It doesn't matter if the book isn't finished that session — it can be finished at home, either by the parents or — even better — by the child who can't wait to see what will happen next. Again, it's easier for a child to read a book when they know what it's about and what the more unusual words in it are going to be.

Series books are excellent for this — if the child falls in love with one of them, they'll really work at reading the next and the next and the next. And be genuinely disappointed when they run out!

# Bag a book from my collection

Hunt out some of these books next time you're at a local library or bookshop.

### Beginning readers
*Diary of a Wombat* • *Pete the Sheep*

### Funny books for young readers
(Also good for older kids who need tempting.)
Wacky Families Series:
*My Dog the Dinosaur* • *My Mum the Pirate*
*My Dad the Dragon* • *My Uncle Gus the Garden Gnome*
*My Uncle Wal the Werewolf* (June 2005)

### Light books
(For when kids have had a long day.)
Phredde series:
*A Phaery Named Phredde* • *Phredde and a Frog Named Bruce*
*Phredde and the Zombie Librarian* • *Phredde and the Temple of Gloom*
*Phredde and the Leopard-Skin Librarian*
*Phredde and the Purple Pyramid* • *Phredde and the Vampire Footy Team*
*Phredde and the Runaway Ghost Train* (Oct 2005)
*Big Burps, Bare Bums and Other Bad-Mannered Blunders*

### Deeper books
(Big but gripping books to tempt kids to read more deeply.)
*Hitler's Daughter* • *Tom Appleby, Convict Boy*
*Dark Wind Blowing* • *Missing You, Love Sara*
*Walking the Boundaries* • *Somewhere Around the Corner*
*Tajore Arkle* • *The White Ship*

### Books for boys

All of the Wacky Family series
*Dark Wind Blowing* • *Soldier on the Hill*
*Hitler's Daughter* • *Walking the Boundaries*
The Outlands trilogy (young adults):
*In the Blood* • *Blood Moon* • *Flesh and Blood*
*A War for Gentlemen* (adults and young adults)

### Books for animal lovers

*The Book of Unicorns*
*Ride the Wild Wind — the golden pony and other stories*
*My Dog the Dinosaur*
*My Uncle Wal the Werewolf* (June 2005)
*Rover, the tale of the dog who discovered America* (Feb 2005)
*The Secret World of Wombats* (Aug 2005)

### Non-fiction books

*How the Aliens From Alpha Centauri Invaded My Maths Class and Turned Me into a Writer*
*How to Guzzle Your Garden* • *The Book of Challenges*
*Stamp, Stomp, Whomp (and other interesting ways to get rid of pests)*
*The Fascinating History of Your Lunch*
*Big Burps, Bare Bums and other Bad-Mannered Blunders*
*To the Moon and Back* (with Bryan Sullivan)
*The Secret World of Wombats* (Aug 2005)
*How to Grow Your Own Spaceship* (Oct 2005)

### Young adults

The Outlands trilogy:
*In the Blood* • *Blood Moon* • *Flesh and Blood*
*A War for Gentlemen*

# About the author

Jackie French's writing career spans 14 years, 39 wombats, 110 books for kids and adults, 15 languages, various awards, radio shows, newspaper and magazine columns, theories of pest and weed ecology and 28 shredded-back doormats. The doormats are the victims of the wombats, who require constant appeasement in the form of carrots, rolled oats and wombat nuts, which is one of the reasons for her prolific output: it pays the carrot bills.

Jackie wrote her first children's book, *Rainstones*, in a desperate attempt to earn enough money to register her car, while living in a shed with a wallaby called Fred, a black snake called Gladys and a wombat called Smudge. The manuscript was described by her publishers as the messiest, worst-spelt manuscript they had ever received.

The 'messiest' was due to Smudge the wombat who left his droppings on the typewriter every night; the spelling was due to the fact she is dyslexic. She recommends all beginning writers to misspell their first book with a wombat-damaged typewriter — at least that way it stands out from the pile!

The book was accepted (and was later shortlisted for the NSW Premier's Award and CBC Younger Reader's Book of the Year). In the same fortnight Jackie was offered a regular column in a newspaper and a farming magazine and discovered that writing about flowers and fantasy was a heck of a lot easier than hauling manure in the old green truck to feed the peach trees. She has been a fulltime writer and wombat negotiator ever since.

Jackie's most recent awards include the 2000 Children's Book Council Book of the Year Award for Younger Readers for the critically acclaimed, *Hitler's Daughter*, which also won the 2002 UK Wow! Award for the most inspiring children's book of the year; the 2002 Aurealis Award for Younger Readers for *Café on Callisto*; ACT Book of the Year for *In the Blood*; and for *Diary of a Wombat* with Bruce Whatley, the Children's Book Council Honour Book, NSW Koala Award for Best Picture Book, Nielsen Book Data/ABA Book of the Year Award, the Cuffie Award for favourite picture book (USA) and the American Literary Association (ALA) for notable children's book.

---

Visit Jackie's website
www.jackiefrench.com
or
www.harpercollins.com.au/jackiefrench
for copies of her monthly newsletter

## TALK, LISTEN AND LEARN by Linda Clark and Catherine Ireland

One of the greatest skills children learn is how to talk and communicate. The development of speech and language provides a foundation for other skills, including how to listen, solve problems, read and write, as well as to speak and socialise with others.

TALK, LISTEN AND LEARN equips parents with clear and practical information on a range of topics.

- The essentials of speech, language and literacy development.
- Fun ways to enhance development at home including the use of toys and music.
- How to help your child through using computers and television.
- Language development in multiple birth and multilingual children.
- How to identify children with speech, language and literacy problems.
- Suggested ways to tackle a range of speech and language problems at home.

www.ingramcontent.com/pod-product-compliance
Lightning Source LLC
Chambersburg PA
CBHW050905300426
44111CB00010B/1393